ISBN 978-1-4234-6218-7

7777 W. BLUEMOUND RD. P.O. BOX 13819 MILWAUKEE, WI 53213

For all works contained herein:
Unauthorized copying, arranging, adapting, recording, Internet posting, public performance,
or other distribution of the printed music in this publication is an infringement of copyright.
Infringers are liable under the law.

Visit Hal Leonard Online at
www.halleonard.com

Contents

How to Use This Book

Piano Chord Songbooks include the lyrics and chords for each song. The melody of the first phrase of each song is also shown.

First, play the melody excerpt to get you started in the correct key. Then, sing the song, playing the chords that are shown above the lyrics.

Chords can be voiced in many different ways. For any chords that are unfamiliar, refer to the diagram that is provided for each chord. It shows the notes that you should play with your right hand. With your left hand, simply play the note that matches the name of the chord. For example, to play a C chord, play C-E-G in your right hand, and play a C in your left hand.

You will notice that some chords are *slash chords*; for example, C/G. With your right hand, play the chord that matches the note on the left side of the slash. With your left hand, play the note on the right side of the slash. So, to play a C/G chord, play a C chord (C-E-G) in your right hand, and play a G in your left hand.

Against All Odds

(Take a Look at Me Now)
from AGAINST ALL ODDS

Words and Music by
Phil Collins

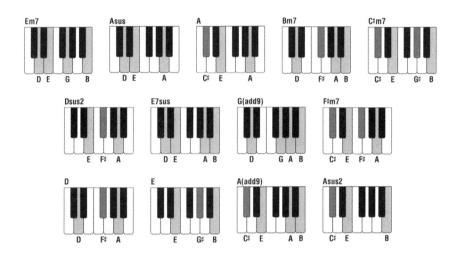

Intro	$\vert$ Em7	$\vert$ Asus A	$\vert$ Em7	$\vert$ Asus A $\vert$

        Bm7   **C♯m7**

Verse 1   How can I just let you walk away,

             Dsus2   **E7sus**

       Just let you leave without a trace?

           G(add9)   **A**   **F♯m7**   **Bm7**

       When I stand here taking ev - 'ry breath with you,   ooh.

           E7sus   **G(add9)**   **Asus A**

       You're the only one who real-ly knew me at all.

© 1984 EMI GOLDEN TORCH MUSIC CORP. and PHILIP COLLINS LTD.
All Rights except Synchronization Rights Jointly Administered by EMI GOLDEN TORCH MUSIC CORP.
and EMI APRIL MUSIC INC. on behalf of PHILIP COLLINS LTD.
Synchronization Rights Exclusively Administered by EMI GOLDEN TORCH MUSIC CORP.
All Rights Reserved   International Copyright Secured   Used by Permission

Verse 2

Bm7   C#m7
How can you just walk away from me,

     Dsus2   E7sus
When all I can do is watch you leave.

      G(add9)   A
'Cause we shared the laughter and__ the pain,

  F#m7   Bm7
And even shared the tears.

     E7sus   G(add9)   Asus A
You're the only one who real-ly knew me at all.

Chorus 1

                    D
So take a look at me now

             E
'Cause there's just an empty space.

      Bm7   G(add9)
There's nothing left here to remind__ me,

    Em7   Asus
Just the mem - 'ry of your face.

   A   D
So take a look at me now,

       E
Well, there's just an empty space,

      Bm7   G(add9)
And you coming back__ to me is against__ the odds,

    Em7   Asus A
And that's what__ I've got to face.

Verse 3

  Bm7   C#m7
I wish I could just make you turn around,

Dsus2   Em7
Turn around and see me cry.

     G(add9)   A
There's so much I need to say__ to you,

  F#m7   Bm7
So many reasons why.

     Em7   G(add9)   Asus A
You're the only one who real-ly knew me at all.

Chorus 2

                                         D
So take a look at me now,

                        E
'Cause there's just an empty space,

                        Bm7   **G(add9)**
And there's nothing left here to remind___ me,

              Em7   **Asus**
Just the mem - 'ry of your face.

              A   **D**
So take a look at me now,

                        E
Still there's just an empty space,

              Bm7   **G(add9)**
But to wait___ for you is all___ I can do,

                        Em7   **Asus**
And that's what___ I've got to face.

                                    D
Take a good look at me now

                    E
'Cause I'll still be standing here,

                        Bm7   **G(add9)**
And you coming back___ to me is against___ all odds.

              Em7   **Asus   A(add9)**
That's the chance I've got to take.

              Em7   **Asus   Asus2   Em7**
Yeah.

A   **Em7**
    Take a look at me now.

| **A** | **G(add9)** | **A(add9)** | |

All I Wanna Do

Words and Music by Kevin Gilbert,
David Baerwald, Sheryl Crow,
Wyn Cooper and Bill Bottrell

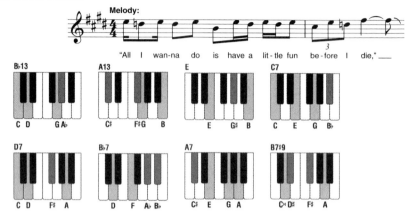

"All   I   wan-na   do   is   have a   lit-tle fun   be-fore   I   die," ___

Intro

Bb13   A13
Hit it!   This ain't no disco.

Bb13   A13
*   It ain't no country club either.*

Bb13   A13
*   This is L.A.*

Verse 1

    E
"All I wanna do is have a little fun before I die,"

        C7   D7
Says the man__ next to me out of nowhere,

E
  Apropos of nothing.

He says his name is William,

C7
  But I'm sure he's Bill,

    D7
Or Billy, or Mac, or Buddy.

       E
And he's   plain ugly to me,

Copyright © 1993 Sony/ATV Music Publishing LLC, Almo Music Corp., Zen Of Iniquity, Warner-Tamerlane Publishing Corp.,
Old Crow Music, WB Music Corp., Canvas Mattress Music and Ignorant Music
All Rights on behalf of Sony/ATV Music Publishing LLC Administered by
Sony/ATV Music Publishing LLC, 8 Music Square West, Nashville, TN 37203
All Rights on behalf of Zen Of Iniquity Administered by Almo Music Corp.
International Copyright Secured   All Rights Reserved

And I wonder if he's ever

C7   **D7**   **E**
Had a day of fun in his whole life.

We are drinking beer at noon on Tuesday

C7   **D7**
In a bar that faces a gi-ant car wash.

E
And the good people of the world

Are washin' their cars on their lunch break,

C7   **D7**   **B♭7**
   Hosing and scrubbing the best they can in skirts and suits.

Pre-Chorus 1   **A7**   **B♭7**
   They drive their shiny Datsuns and Buicks

           A7   **B♭7**
   Back to the phone company, the record store, too.

           A7
   We'll they're nothing like Billy 'n' me.

Chorus 1   **E**
   'Cause all I wanna do is have some fun,

           C7   **D7**
I got a feel - in' I'm not the only one.

           E
All I wanna do is have some fun,

           C7   **D7**
I got a feel - in' I'm not the only one.

           E
All I wanna do is have some fun,

      C7
Until the sun comes up

       B7♯9   **E**   **C7**   **D7**
Over Santa Monica Boulevard.

Verse 2

E
 I like a good beer buzz early in the morning,

C7   D7
And Billy likes to peel the labels from his bottles of Bud.

E
 He shreds them on the bar,

                                         C7
Then he lights ev'ry match in an oversized__ pack,

         D7   E
Letting each one__ burn down to his thick fingers

Before blowin' and cursin' them out.

C7   D7   B♭7
 He's watchin' the bottles of Bud as they spin on the floor.

Pre-Chorus 2

A7   B♭7
 And a happy couple enters the bar

A7   B♭7
 Dang'rously close to one another.

A7
 The bartender looks up from his want ads.

Chorus 2   **Repeat Chorus 1**

Interlude | E | | C7 | D7 |
                     | E | | C7 | D7   B♭7 |

Bridge

A7   Bb7
Otherwise the bar is ours,

A7   Bb7
The day and the night and the car wash, too.

A7
The matches and the Buds

                       Bb7
And the clean and dirty cars,

A7
The sun and the moon.

Chorus 3

                    E
But all I wanna do is have some fun.

             C7   D7
I got a feel - in' I'm not the only one.

            E
All I wanna do is have some fun.

             C7   D7
I got a feel - in' I'm not the only one.

            E
All I wanna do is have some fun.

            C7   D7
I got a feel - in' the party has just begun.

                 E
All I wanna do is have some fun.

             C7   **D7**
I won't tell__ ya that you're the only one.

                 E
All I wanna do is have some fun,

             C7
Until the sun comes up

       D7   **E**
Over Santa Monica Boulevard,

             C7
Until the sun comes up

       B7♯9   **E**
Over Santa Monica Boulevard.

Outro | E | | C7 | D7 |
                | E | | C7 | D7 |
                | E | | C7 | B7♯9 |
                | E | | | |

All Out of Love

Words and Music by Graham Russell
and Clive Davis

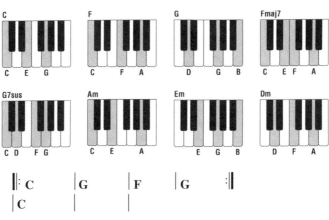

Intro

‖: C | G | F | G :‖

| C | | |

Verse 1

    F   C
I'm lying alone with my head on the phone,

 F   C
Thinking of you 'til it hurts.

   F   G
I know you hurt too, but what else can we do,

   F   Fmaj7 G7sus
Tor-mented and torn apart.

   F   C
I wish I could carry your smile__ in my heart,

   F   C
For times when my life seems so low.

     F   G
It would make me believe what to-morrow could bring,

     F   Fmaj7   G7sus   G
When to-day doesn't really know,   doesn't real - ly know.

Chorus 1

     C   G
I'm all out of love, I'm so lost without you,

    F   F   G
I know you were right, believ - ing for so__ long.

Copyright © 1980 by Nottsongs
All Rights Administered by Universal Music - Careers
International Copyright Secured All Rights Reserved

```
          C                G
I'm all out of love, what am I without you?

          F                          G          C
I can't be too late to say that I was__ so wrong.


          F                    C
I want you to come back and carry me home,

            F                          C
A-way from these long, lonely nights.

            F                    G
I'm reaching for you. Are you feeling it too?

              F                          Fmaj7   G7sus
Does the feeling seem oh, so right?

            F                    C
And what would you say if I called on you now,

            F                    C
And said that I can't hold on?

              F                    G
There's no easy way, it gets harder each day,

              F                    Fmaj7              G7sus  G
Please love me or I'll be gone,     I'll be gone.
```

Verse 2 (beside "I want you to come back...")

Chorus 2   **Repeat Chorus 1**

```
              Am Em                      F    Em
Oo. What are you thinking of?

              Dm                    Am
What are you thinking of?

              Em                    F    Em
What are you thinking of?

              Dm                    F    G
What are you thinking of?
```

Bridge (beside "Oo. What are you thinking of?")

```
              C
I'm all out of love,

              G
I'm so lost without you.
```

Chorus 3 (beside "I'm all out of love,")

F
I know you were right

     F   **G**
Believ - ing for so__ long.

     C
I'm all out of love.

     G
What am I without you?

    F
I can't be too late.

       G
I know I was so__ wrong.

Chorus 4   *Repeat Chorus 3*

     C
Chorus 5   I'm all out of love,

     G
I'm so lost without you.

    F
I know you were right

     F   **G**
Believ - ing for so__ long.

     C
I'm all out of love.

     G
What am I without you?

    F
I can't be too late

       G   **C**
To say that I was__ so wrong.

I'm all out of love.

     G
I'm so lost without you.

    F   **G** **C**
I know you were right.

Alone

Words and Music by Billy Steinberg
and Tom Kelly

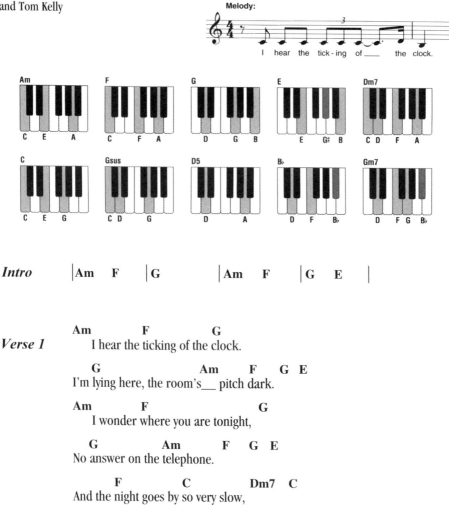

Melody:

I hear the tick-ing of ___ the clock.

Intro |Am F |G |Am F |G E |

Verse 1
    Am   F   G
I hear the ticking of the clock.

G   Am   F G E
I'm lying here, the room's__ pitch dark.

Am   F   G
I wonder where you are tonight,

G   Am   F G E
No answer on the telephone.

   F   C   Dm7 C
And the night goes by so very slow,

   F   C   Dm7 Gsus
Oh, I hope that it won't end, though,

G   C
Alone.

Copyright © 1983 Sony/ATV Music Publishing LLC
All Rights Administered by Sony/ATV Music Publishing LLC, 8 Music Square West, Nashville, TN 37203
International Copyright Secured   All Rights Reserved

Chorus 1

D5   Bb   F   C   D5
     'Til now I always got by on my own,

Bb   F   C   D5
I never really cared until I met you.

Bb   F   C
    And now it chills me to the bone.

F   Bb   C
How do I get you alone?

F   Bb   C
How do I get you alone?

Verse 2

Am   F   G
    You don't know how long I have wanted

  G   Am   F G   E
To touch your lips and hold you tight.   Oh.

Am   F   G
    You don't know how long I have waited,

  G   Am   F   G E
And I was gonna tell you tonight.

       F   C   Dm7 C
But the secret is still my own,

       F   C   Dm7 Gsus
And my love for you is still unknown,

G   C
Alone.

D5 Bb F C D5   Bb F   C
                      Oh, oh,   whoa.

Chorus 2

   D5   B♭   F   C   D5
          'Til now I always got by on my own,

B♭   F   C   D5
I never really cared until I met you.

B♭   F   C
     And now it chills me to the bone.

F   B♭   C
How do I get you alone?

F   B♭   C
How do I get you alone?

Solo

D5 B♭	F C	D5 B♭	F C	
F C	B♭ F	Gm7 F	C	
C				

Chorus 3

  F   B♭   C
How do I get you alone?

  F   B♭   C
How do I get you alone,

    F   B♭ C
A-lone,

    F   B♭ C
A-lone?

| Am   F | G | Am |

Bad Day

Words and Music by
Daniel Powter

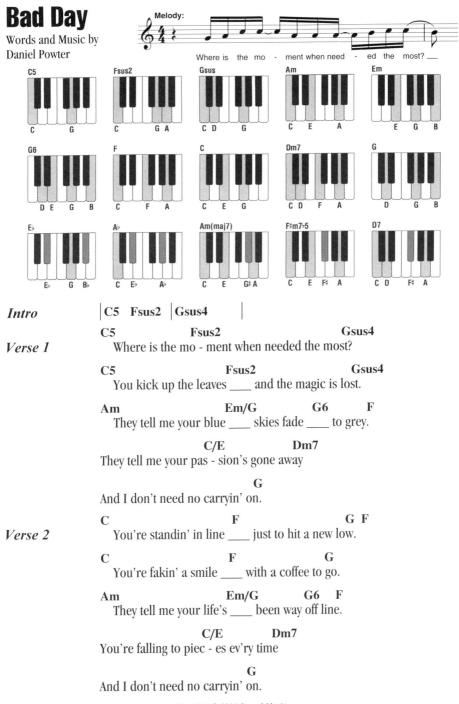

Intro

| C5 Fsus2 | Gsus4 | |

Verse 1

C5   Fsus2   Gsus4
Where is the mo - ment when needed the most?

C5   Fsus2   Gsus4
You kick up the leaves ___ and the magic is lost.

Am   Em/G   G6   F
They tell me your blue ___ skies fade ___ to grey.

          C/E   Dm7
They tell me your pas - sion's gone away

            G
And I don't need no carryin' on.

Verse 2

C   F   G F
You're standin' in line ___ just to hit a new low.

C   F   G
You're fakin' a smile ___ with a coffee to go.

Am   Em/G   G6 F
They tell me your life's ___ been way off line.

         C/E   Dm7
You're falling to piec - es ev'ry time

            G
And I don't need no carryin' on.

Copyright © 2006 Song 6 Music
All Rights Administered by Sony/ATV Music Publishing LLC, 8 Music Square West, Nashville, TN 37203
International Copyright Secured   All Rights Reserved

Chorus 1

N.C.   C   F
Because you had a bad day. You're takin' one down.

         Dm7   G
You sing a sad song just to turn it around.

         C   F
You say you don't know. You tell me don't lie.

         Dm7   G
You work at a smile ____ and you go for a ride.

         Am   Em/G
You had a bad day. The cam'ra don't lie.

         F   C/E
You're comin' back down and you really don't mind.

         Dm7
You had a bad day.

G   C5 Fsus2 Gsus4 F C5 Fsus2 Gsus4 G
 You had a bad day.

Bridge 1

Am   Em/G   F
 Well, you need a blue ____ sky holiday.

         C/E   Dm7
The point is they laugh ____ at what you say

         Gsus4 G
And I don't need no carryin' on.

Chorus 2

         C   F
You had a bad day. You're takin' one down.

         Dm7   G
You sing a sad song just to turn it around.

         C   F
You say you don't know. You tell me don't lie.

         Dm7   G
You work at a smile ____ and you go for a ride.

         Am   Em/G
You had a bad day. The cam'ra don't lie.

         F   C/E
You're comin' back down and you really don't mind.

         Dm7   C/E
You had a bad day. ____ Oh, on a holiday.

Bridge 2

E♭
Sometimes the system goes on the blink

A♭
And the whole thing, it turns out wrong.

E♭
You might not make it back

A♭
And you know that you could be, well,

Gsus4   G
All that strong and I'm not wrong, ___ yeah.

Verse 3

C5   Fsus2   Gsus4
  So where is the pas - sion when you need it the most?

C5   Fsus2   G
Oh, you and I. ___You kick up the leaves ___ and the magic is lost.

Chorus 3

N.C.   C   F
'Cause you had a bad day. You're takin' one down.

Dm7   G
You sing a sad song just to turn it around.

C   F
You say you don't know. You tell me don't lie.

Dm7   G
You work at a smile ___ and you go for a ride.

Am   Am(maj7)/G♯
You had a bad day. You've seen what you like.

Am/G   F♯m7♭5
And how does it feel ___ one more time?

D7   F Gsus4   C F Dm7 G
You had a bad day. You had a bad day.

Outro

‖: C   F |Dm7 G :‖ *Repeat and fade w/ Vocal ad lib.*

Best of My Love

Words and Music by John David Souther,
Don Henley and Glenn Frey

Melody:

Ev - er - y   night __   I'm   ly - in'   in   bed __

Intro ‖: Cmaj7add2   C |Cmaj7add2   C |
|Fmaj7#11   Fmaj7 |Fmaj7#11   Fmaj7   :‖

Verse 1

Cmaj7 C
Ev - ery night

Cmaj7 C
I'm ly - in' in bed

Fmaj7♭5 Fmaj7   Fmaj7♭5 Fmaj7
Hold - in' you close in my dreams;

Cmaj7 C
Think - in' about all the things that we said

  F
And comin' apart at the seams.

Em7   Dm7
  We tried to talk it o - ver

    Em7   F
But the words come out too rough.

  Cmaj7 C
I know you were tryin'

  Fmaj7   Cmaj7 C   G G7 G6 G7
To give me the best of your love.

© 1974 (Renewed 2002) EMI BLACKWOOD MUSIC INC., CASS COUNTY MUSIC and RED CLOUD MUSIC
All Rights Reserved   International Copyright Secured   Used by Permission

Verse 2

Cmaj7 C
Beau - tiful faces,

Cmaj7 C
An' loud empty places.

Fmaj7♭5 Fmaj7   Fmaj7♭5 Fmaj7
  Look at the way that we live,

Cmaj7 C
Wast - in' our time

On cheap talk and wine

F
  Left us so little to give.

Em7
The same old crowd

      Dm7
Was like a cold dark cloud

   Em7   F
That we could never rise above,

   Cmaj7 C
But here   in my heart

 Fmaj7   Cmaj7 C G G7 G6 G7
I give you the best of my love.

           C
Chorus 1   Whoa,__ sweet darlin',

                     F
You get the best of my love,

(You get the best of my love.)

      Cmaj7
Whoa,__ sweet darlin',

                    F
You get the best of my love.

(You get the best of my love.)

Bridge

       Fm
Oo, I'm goin' back in time

       Cmaj7
And it's a sweet dream.

        Fm
It was a quiet night

And I would be alright

       Dm7 G7
If I could go on sleeping.

Verse 3

      Cmaj7 C
But ev - ery morning

     Cmaj7 C
I wake up and worry

  Fmaj7♭5 F
        What's gonna happen today.

Cmaj7 C
You   see it your way,

     Cmaj7 C
And I   see it mine,

    F
But we both see it slippin' away.

Em7   **Dm7**
   You know, we always had each other, baby.

Em7   **F**
   I guess that wasn't e-nough.

     Cmaj7 C
Oh, but here   in my heart

   Fmaj7   **Cmaj7 C**   **G**
I give you the best of my love.

Chorus 2   ***Repeat Chorus 1 till fade***

Come Sail Away

Words and Music by
Dennis DeYoung

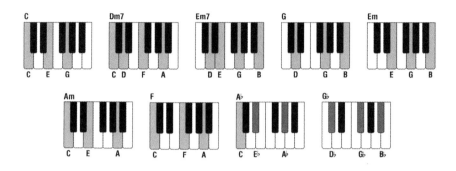

Intro | C | Dm7 | Em7 |
             | Dm7 | C | G |

Verse 1

    C Em   Am G F
I'm sailing a-way,

                      G
Set an open course for the virgin sea.

    C   Em   Am   G F
As I've got to be free,

                      G
Free to face the life that's a-head of me.

Am   G
  On board I'm the captain,   so climb aboard.

Am   G
  We'll search for tomorrow   on ev'ry shore.

      C Em   Am G F
And I'll try, oh Lord, I'll try

      G   C Dm7 Em7 Dm7 C   G
To car - ry on.

Copyright © 1977 ALMO MUSIC CORP. and STYGIAN SONGS
Copyright Renewed
All Rights Controlled and Administered by ALMO MUSIC CORP.
All Rights Reserved Used by Permission

Verse 2
    C Em   **Am** **G** **F**
I look to the sea,

                                 G
Reflections in the waves spark my memory.

C   **Em**   **Am** **G** **F**
Some happy, some sad.

                               G
I think of childhood friends, and the dreams we had.

Am   **G**
   We live happily forever,   so the story goes.

Am   **G**
   But somehow we missed out   on a pot of gold.

         C   **Em**   **Am** **G F**
But we'll___ try best that we can

         G   **C**
To car - ry on.

Interlude 1 ‖: **C** | **F** | **G** | **F**   :‖

Pre-Chorus
        C   **F**
A gathering of angels

      G   **F**
Ap-peared above my head.

       C   **F**
They sang to me this song of hope.

      G   **F**
And this is what they said,   they said

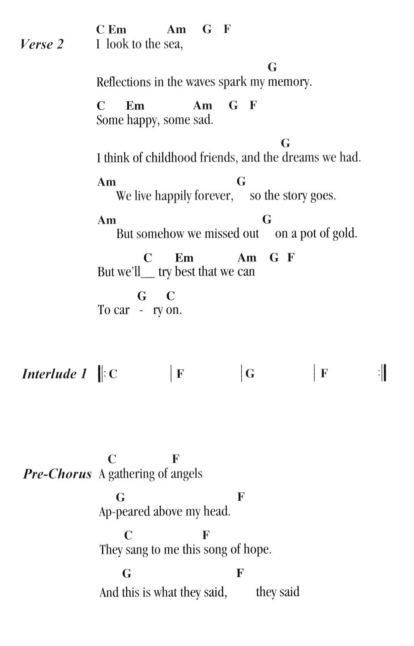

Chorus 1

      C   F
Come sail away, come sail away,

          G   F
Come sail away with me, lads.

      C   F
Come sail away, come sail away,

          G   F
Come sail away with me.

      C   F
Come sail away, come sail away,

          G   F
Come sail away with me, baby.

      C   F
Come sail away, come sail away,

          G   A♭
Come sail away with me.

Interlude 2 ‖: A♭ | G♭   :‖   ***Play 15 times***
        A♭ | | |
      ‖: C | F | G | F   :‖ ***Play 3 times***

Pre-Chorus

      C   F
I thought that they were angels,

      G   F
But to my sur-prise.

        C   F
We climbed aboard their starship,

      G   F
We headed for the skies. (Singin'...)

Chorus 2   ***Repeat Chorus 1 till fade***

Borderline

Words and Music by
Reggie Lucas

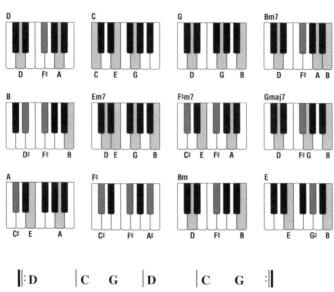

Intro   ‖: D |C   G |D |C   G   :‖

Verse 1
D   C   G   D C G
Somethin' in the way you love__ me won't__ let me be.

       G   D
I don't__ wan - na be your pris'ner,

       C   G   D   C G
So ba - by, won't you set me free.

       G   D   C   G
Stop__ play - in' with my heart. Fin - ish what you start

       D   C G
When__ you make my love come down.

       G   D
If you__ want__ me let me know.

      C   G
Ba - by, let it show.

      D
Hon - ey, don't you fool around.

Copyright © 1984 by Universal Music - Careers
International Copyright Secured All Rights Reserved

Pre-Chorus 1

    Bm7   B   Em7
     Just try to under-stand,

      A   F♯m7
  I've given all I can,

        Gmaj7   G   A
  'Cause you got the best of me.

Chorus 1

  A   F♯
  Borderline,

      Bm   A   E
  Feels like I'm go - in' to lose__ my mind.

      Em7   D
  You just keep__ on pushin' my love

     D   A   D A
  Over the bor - derline.

  A   F♯
  Borderline,

      Bm   A   E
  Feels like I'm go - in' to lose my mind.

      Em7   D
  You just keep__ on pushin' my love

     D   A   D A
  Over the bor - derline.

  A   F♯
  Keep on pushin' me, baby.

      Bm   A   E
  Don't you know__ you drive me crazy?

      Em7   D
  You just keep__ on pushin' my love

     D   A   D A
  Over the bor - derline.

Interlude   **Repeat Intro**

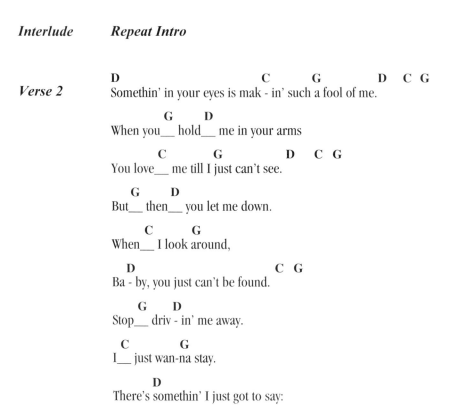

Verse 2

D   C   G   D C G
Somethin' in your eyes is mak - in' such a fool of me.

        G   D
When you___ hold___ me in your arms

        C   G   D C G
You love___ me till I just can't see.

     G   D
But___ then___ you let me down.

     C   G
When___ I look around,

   D   C G
Ba - by, you just can't be found.

     G   D
Stop___ driv - in' me away.

   C   G
I___ just wan-na stay.

        D
There's somethin' I just got to say:

Pre-Chorus 2 **Repeat Pre-Chorus 1**

Chorus 2   *Repeat Chorus 1*

Chorus 3

     A   F♯   Bm
      Look what your love has done to me.

          A   E
Come on, baby, set me free.

            Em7   D
You just keep___ on pushin' my love

          D   A   D A
Over the bor - derline.

A   F♯
      You cause me so much pain

               Bm
I think I'm goin' insane.

          A   E
What does it take to make you see?

           Em7   D
You just keep___ on pushin' my love

          D   A   D A
Over the bor - derline.

Chorus 4   *Repeat Chorus 3 till fade*

Clocks

Words and Music by Guy Berryman,
Jon Buckland, Will Champion and Chris Martin

Lights go out and I can't be saved, ___

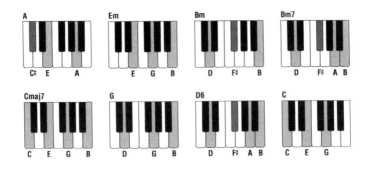

Intro ‖: A |Em | |Bm :‖ *Play 4 times*

Verse 1

    A   **Em**
Lights go out and I can't be saved,

                  Bm7
Tides that I tried to swim ___ against

      A   **Em**
Have brought me down up - on my knees,

   Bm7
Oh, I beg, I beg and plead.

       A   **Em**   **Bm7**
Singing: come out of things unsaid, shoot an apple off my head.

       A   **Em**   **Bm7**
And a   trouble that can't be named, a tiger's waiting to be tamed.

Chorus 1

          A   **Em**   **Bm**
Singing: You ___ are.

  A   **Em**   **Bm**
  You ___ are.

Interlude 1 ‖: A |Em | |Bm :‖

Copyright © 2002 by Universal Music Publishing MGB Ltd.
All Rights in the United States Administered by Universal Music - MGB Songs
International Copyright Secured   All Rights Reserved

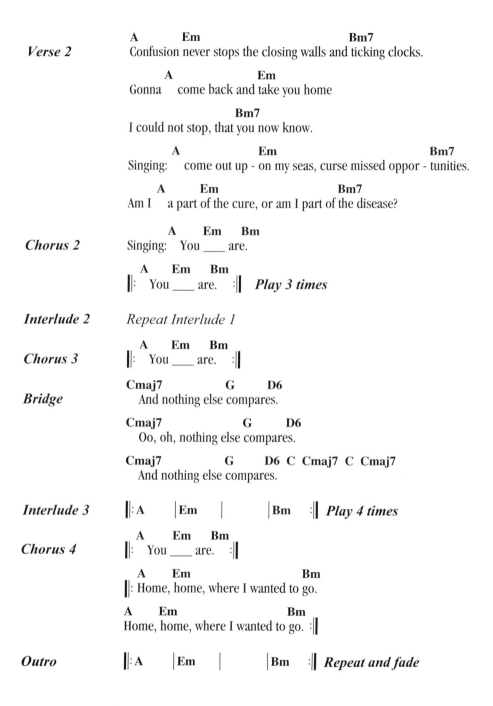

Verse 2

     A   Em   Bm7
Confusion never stops the closing walls and ticking clocks.

        A   Em
Gonna   come back and take you home

                 Bm7
I could not stop, that you now know.

         A   Em   Bm7
Singing: come out up - on my seas, curse missed oppor - tunities.

       A   Em   Bm7
Am I   a part of the cure, or am I part of the disease?

Chorus 2

       A   Em   Bm
Singing: You ___ are.

   A   Em   Bm
‖: You ___ are. :‖   *Play 3 times*

Interlude 2   *Repeat Interlude 1*

Chorus 3

   A   Em   Bm
‖: You ___ are. :‖

Bridge

Cmaj7   G   D6
  And nothing else compares.

Cmaj7   G   D6
  Oo, oh, nothing else compares.

Cmaj7   G   D6 C Cmaj7 C Cmaj7
  And nothing else compares.

Interlude 3   ‖: A |Em | |Bm :‖ *Play 4 times*

Chorus 4

   A   Em   Bm
‖: You ___ are. :‖

   A   Em   Bm
‖: Home, home, where I wanted to go.

A   Em   Bm
Home, home, where I wanted to go. :‖

Outro   ‖: A |Em | |Bm :‖ *Repeat and fade*

Crazy Little Thing Called Love

Words and Music by
Freddie Mercury

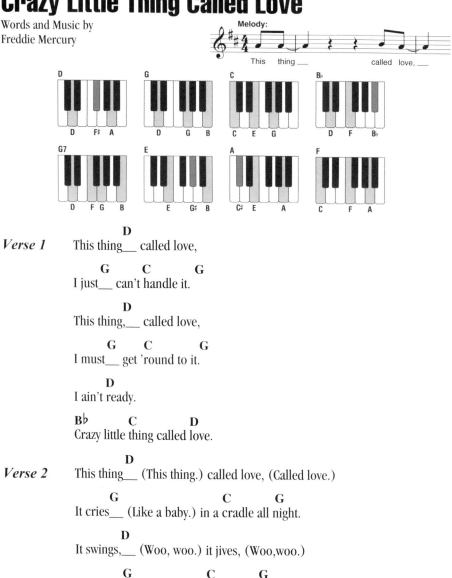

Verse 1

          D
This thing__ called love,

     G   **C**   **G**
I just__ can't handle it.

          D
This thing,__ called love,

     G   **C**   **G**
I must__ get 'round to it.

          D
I ain't ready.

B♭   **C**   **D**
Crazy little thing called love.

Verse 2

          D
This thing__ (This thing.) called love, (Called love.)

     G   **C**   **G**
It cries__ (Like a baby.) in a cradle all night.

          D
It swings,__ (Woo, woo.) it jives, (Woo,woo.)

     G   **C**   **G**
It shakes__ all over like a jellyfish.

          D
I kinda like it.

B♭   **C**   **D**
Crazy little thing called love.

© 1979 QUEEN MUSIC LTD.
All Rights for the U.S. and Canada Controlled and Administered by BEECHWOOD MUSIC CORP.
All Rights for the world excluding the U.S. and Canada Controlled and Administered by EMI MUSIC PUBLISHING LTD.
All Rights Reserved   International Copyright Secured   Used by Permission

Bridge 1
                G7
There goes my baby,

       C   **G**
She knows how to rock 'n' roll.

            B♭
She drives me crazy.

           E   **A**
She gives me hot and cold fever,

        F   **N.C.**   **E**
Then she leaves me in a cool, cool sweat.

Verse 3
    A   **D**
    I gotta be cool,__ relax,

      G   **C**   **G**
Get hip,__ get on my tracks,

      D
Take the back seat, hitch hike,

      G   **C**   **G**
And take a long ride on my motor-bike

      D
Until I'm ready.

B♭   **C**   **D**
Crazy little thing called love.

Bridge 2   ***Repeat Bridge 1***

Verse 4   ***Repeat Verse 3***

Verse 5   ***Repeat Verse 1***

Outro
       B♭   **C**   **D**
‖: Crazy little thing called love. :‖ ***Repeat and fade***

Don't Know Why

Words and Music by
Jesse Harris

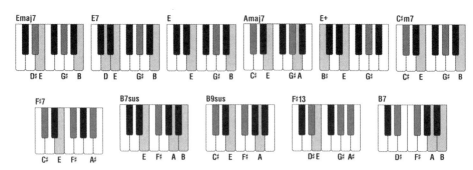

Intro | Emaj7 E7 E | Amaj7 E+ | C#m7 F#7 B7sus4 | B9sus4 |

Verse 1
Emaj7 E7 E   Amaj7   E+
I   waited till I ___ saw ___ the sun.

C#m7   F#7 B7sus4   E
I don't know why ___ I did - n't come.

Emaj7   E7 E   Amaj7   E+
I left you by ___ the house ___ of fun.

C#m7   F#7 B7sus4   E
I don't know why ___ I did - n't come,

C#m7   F#7 B7sus4   E
I   don't know why ___ I did - n't come.

Verse 2
Emaj7   E7   E   Amaj7   E+
When I saw ___ the break ___ of day,

C#m7   F#7   B7sus4   E
I wished that I ___ could fly ___ away

Emaj7   E7   E Amaj7   E+
'Stead of kneel - ing in ___ the sand

C#m7   F#7   B7sus4 E
Catching tear - drops in my hand.

Copyright © 2002 Sony/ATV Music Publishing LLC and Beanly Songs
All Rights Administered by Sony/ATV Music Publishing LLC, 8 Music Square West, Nashville, TN 37203
International Copyright Secured   All Rights Reserved

Bridge 1

C#m7   F#13 B7
My heart is drenched ____ in wine,

  C#m7 F#13   B7 B7/A B7/G# B7/F#
But you'll be on ____ my mind ____ for - ev - er.

Verse 3

  Emaj7 E7 E   Amaj7 E+
  Out across ____ the end - less sea,

C#m7   F#7 B7sus4 E
I would die ____ in ecstasy.

Emaj7 E7 E   Amaj7   E+
But I'll be ____ a bag ____ of bones

C#m7   F#7   B7sus4 E
Driving down ____ the road ____ alone.

Bridge 2

C#m7   F#13   B7
My heart is drenched ____ in wine,

  C#m7 F#13   B7
But you'll be on ____ my mind ____ forever.

Piano Solo

‖: Emaj7 E7 E │Amaj7 E+ │C#m7 F#7 B9sus4 │   :‖

Verse 4

Emaj7   E7 E   Amaj7 E+
Something has ____ to make ____ you run.

C#m7   F#7 B7sus4 E
I don't know why ____ I did - n't come.

 Emaj7 E7 E Amaj7   E+
I feel as empty ____ as ____ a drum.

C#m7   F#7 B7sus4 E
I don't know why ____ I did - n't come,

 C#m7   F#7 B7sus4 E
I don't know why ____ I did - n't come.

 C#m7   F#7 B7sus4 E
I ____ don't know why ____ I did - n't come.

Dreams

Words and Music by
Stevie Nicks

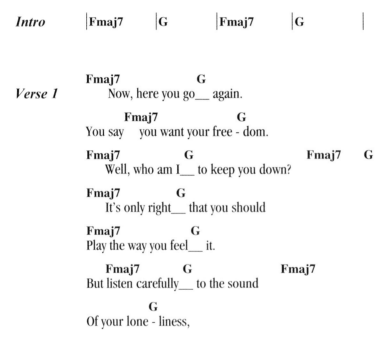

Intro |Fmaj7 |G |Fmaj7 |G |

Verse 1

Fmaj7   **G**
    Now, here you go__ again.

     Fmaj7   **G**
You say   you want your free - dom.

Fmaj7   **G**   **Fmaj7**   **G**
    Well, who am I__ to keep you down?

Fmaj7   **G**
    It's only right__ that you should

Fmaj7   **G**
Play the way you feel__ it.

   Fmaj7   **G**   **Fmaj7**
But listen carefully__ to the sound

       G
Of your lone - liness,

Copyright © 1977 Welsh Witch Music
Copyright Renewed
All Rights Administered by Sony/ATV Music Publishing, 8 Music Square West, Nashville, TN 37203
International Copyright Secured   All Rights Reserved

Fmaj7   G
Like a heartbeat, drives you mad,

    F   G
In the still - ness of remem-bering

      Fmaj7 G   Fmaj7 G
What you had   and what you lost,

        Fmaj7 G   Fmaj7 G
And what you had   and what you lost.

      Fmaj7   G   Fmaj7 G
Chorus 1 Oh, thunder only hap - pens when it's rain - ing.

Fmaj7   G   Fmaj7 G
Players only love__ you when they're play - ing.

    Fmaj7   G   Fmaj7 G
Say, women, they will come__ and they will go.

Fmaj7   G   Fmaj7 G
When the rain washes__ you clean, you'll know.

    Fmaj7
You'll know.

Solo | Fmaj7 | G | Fmaj7 | |
     | Am G| | Fmaj7 | |

Verse 2
Fmaj7   G
Now, here I go__ again.

Fmaj7   G
I see   the crystal vis - ions.

Fmaj7   G   Fmaj7   G
I keep my vis - ions to myself.

Fmaj7   G
It's only me__ who wants to

Fmaj7   G
Wrap around your dreams.

Fmaj7   G   Fmaj7
And have you any dreams__ you'd like to sell?

G   Fmaj7   G
Dreams of lone - liness, like a heartbeat, drives you mad,

Fmaj7   G
In the still - ness of remem-bering

Fmaj7 G   Fmaj7   G
What you had   and what you lost

Fmaj7 G   Fmaj7   G
And what you had   and what you lost.

Chorus 2   **Repeat Chorus 1**

Outro
G   Fmaj7
You will know.

G   Fmaj7
Oh,__ you'll know.

Every Breath You Take

Music and Lyrics by
Sting

Melody:

Ev - 'ry breath you ___ take,

G | Em | C | D | Dsus
D | G B | E G B | C E G | D F♯ A | D G A

D7sus | Am7 | A7 | E♭ | F
C D G A | C E G A | C♯ E G A | E♭ G B♭ | C F A

Intro | G | | Em | | |
| C | D | G | | |

Verse 1
           G
Ev'ry breath you take,

           Em
Ev'ry move you make,

           C
Ev'ry bond you break,

           D
Ev'ry step you take,

           Em
I'll be watching you.

Verse 2
D7sus **G**
Ev'ry single day,

           Em
Ev'ry word you say,

           C
Ev'ry game you play,

           D
Ev'ry night you stay,

      Dsus **G**
I'll be watch-ing you.

© 1983 G.M. SUMNER
Administered by EMI MUSIC PUBLISHING LIMITED
All Rights Reserved   International Copyright Secured   Used by Permission

Bridge 1

        C
Oh, can't you see

        Am7   **G**
You be-long to me?

        A7
How my poor heart__ aches

        D
With ev'ry step you take.

Verse 3

        D7sus   **G**
Ev'ry move you make,

        Em
Ev'ry vow you break,

        C
Ev'ry smile you fake,

        D
Ev'ry claim you stake,

        Dsus   **Em**
I'll be watch-ing you.

Bridge 2

E♭
Since you've gone,

I've been lost without a trace,

F
I dream at night I can only see your face.

E♭
I look around, but it's you I can't replace.

F
I feel so cold and I long for your embrace.

E♭   **G**
I keep crying, baby, baby, please.

Interlude

G		Em		
C	D	Em		D
G		Em		
C	D	G		

Bridge 3   **Repeat Bridge 1**

Verse 4

      D7sus   **G**
Ev'ry move you make,

         Em
Ev'ry vow you break,

           C
Ev'ry smile you fake,

          D
Ev'ry claim you stake,

      Dsus   **Em**
I'll be watch-ing you.

           C
Ev'ry move you make,

         D
Ev'ry step you take,

      Dsus   **Em**
I'll be watch-ing you.

Outro

      D7sus   **G**
I'll be watching you.

  G
‖:   Ev'ry breath you take, ev'ry move you make,

Em   **C**
    Ev'ry bond you break,   ev'ry step you take,

G
    Ev'ry single day, ev'ry word you say,

Em   **C**
  Ev'ry game you play,   ev'ry night you stay. :‖ *Repeat and fade*

Give a Little Bit

Words and Music by Rick Davies
and Roger Hodgson

Melody:

Give a lit - tle bit, ___

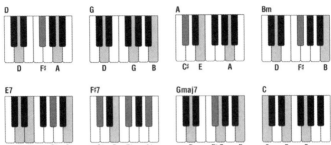

Verse 1

D
Give a little bit,

        G   A   G A G
Give a little bit of your love__ to me.

D   A
I'll give a little bit,

D   G   A   G A G
I'll give a little bit of my love__ to you.

Bm   E7
There's so much that we need__ to share,

G   Bm/A A   D A
So send a smile and show__ you care.

Verse 2

D   A
I'll give a little bit,

D   G   A   G A G
I'll give a little bit of my life__ for you.

D   A
So, give a little bit,

D   G   A   G A G
Oh, give a little bit of your time__ to me.

Bm   E7
See the man with the lone - ly eyes?

G   Bm/A A   D A
Oh, take his hand, you'll be sur - prised.

Copyright © 1977 ALMO MUSIC CORP. and DELICATE MUSIC
Copyright Renewed
All Rights Controlled and Administered by ALMO MUSIC CORP.
All Rights Reserved Used by Permission

Solo ‖:F♯7 |Gmaj7   :‖
        |C G |A D |A | D |A |

Verse 3

    D
      Give a little bit,

                  G   **A**   **G A G**
    Give a little bit of your love___ to me.

    D   **A**
      I'll give a little bit,

    D   **G**   **A**   **G A G**
      I'll give a little bit of my life___ to you.

    Bm   **E7**
      Now's the time that we need___ to share,

     G
    So find yourself,

       C   **G**   **A**   **D**
    We're on our way back home.

    A   **D**   **A**   **D**
      Oh,___ goin' home.

    A   **D**   **A**   **D**
      Don't you need, don't you need to feel at home?

    A   **D**   **G A G D**
      Oh, yeah,___ we gotta sing.

Give Me One Reason

Words and Music by
Tracy Chapman

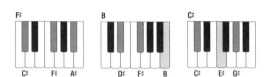

Intro

F#	B C#	F#		
B	C#	F#		
C#	B	F#		

Verse 1

F#
Give me one reason to stay here

B   C#   F#
    And I'll__ turn right back a-round.

B
Give me one reason to stay here

      C#   F#
And I'll__ turn right back a-round.

      C#
Said I don't wanna leave you lonely,

B   F#
    You got to make me change my mind.

© 1996 EMI APRIL MUSIC INC. and PURPLE RABBIT MUSIC
All Rights Controlled and Administered by EMI APRIL MUSIC INC.
All Rights Reserved   International Copyright Secured   Used by Permission

Verse 2

F#
Baby, I got your number,

B   C#   F#
Oh, and I know that a you got mine.

B
You know that I called you,

C#   F#
I call too many times.

        C#
You can call me baby,

        B
You can call me anytime.

        F#
You got to call me.

Verse 3

F#
Give me one reason to stay here

B   C#   F#
And I'll__ turn right back a-round.

(You can see the turn in me.)

Give me one reason to stay here

B   C#   F#
And I'll__ turn right back a-round.

(You can see the turn in me.)

     C#
Said I don't wanna leave you lonely,

B   F#
You got to make me change my mind.

Verse 4   F♯

I don't want no one to squeeze me,

B   C♯   F♯

They might take away my life.

I don't want no one to squeeze me,

B   C♯   F♯

They might take away my life.

       C♯

I just want someone to hold me,

B   F♯

Oh, and rock me through the night.

Interlude   **Repeat Verse 4 (Instrumental)**

Verse 5   F♯

This youthful heart can love you,

B   C♯   F♯

Yes, and give you what you need.

         B

I said this youthful heart can love you,

C♯   F♯

Ho, and give you what you need.

         C♯

But I'm too old to go chasin' you around,

B   F♯

Wastin' my precious energy.

Verse 6

F#
Give me one reason to stay here,

B   C#   F#
Yes, now turn right back a-round.

(Around. You can see the turn in me.)

Give me one reason to stay here,

B   C#   F#
Oh, I'll turn right back a-round.

(You can see the turn in me.)

C#
Said I don't wanna leave you lonely,

B   F#
You got to make me change my mind.

Verse 7

F#
Baby, just give me one reason,

B   C#   F#
Oh, give me just one reason why.

B
Baby, just give me one reason,

C#   F#
Oh, give me just one reason why,

I should stay.

C#
Said I told you that I loved you,

B N.C.   F#
And there ain't no more to say.

Hard Habit to Break

Words and Music by Stephen Kipner
and John Lewis Parker

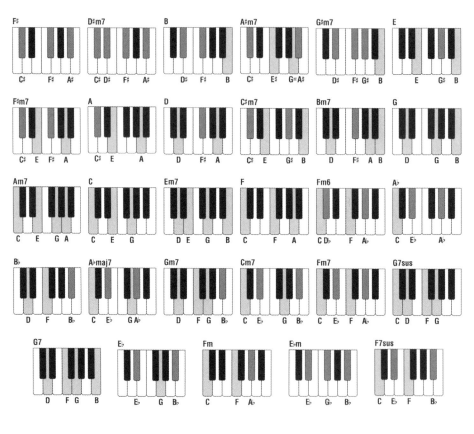

Intro | F♯ | | D♯m7 | |

Verse 1
    F♯
I guess I thought you'd be here forever,

    D♯m7
    Another illusion I chose to create.

       B   **A♯m7**   **D♯m7**
You don't know what you got un-til it's gone,

© 1984 EMI APRIL MUSIC INC., STEPHEN A. KIPNER MUSIC and SONGS OF UNIVERSAL, INC.
All Rights for STEPHEN A. KIPNER MUSIC Controlled and Administered by EMI APRIL MUSIC INC.
All Rights Reserved   International Copyright Secured   Used by Permission

G#m7   E

And I found out a little too late.

F#m7 E   A

I   was   acting as if

                         F#m7

You were lucky to have me,

Doin' you a favor

(I hardly knew you were there.)

    D

But then you were gone,

    C#m7   F#m7

And it all was wrong,

   Bm7   G Am7 G

Had no idea how much I cared.

     C

Chorus 1   Now being without you

       Em

Takes a lot of getting used to,

F

  Should learn to live with it

Fm6

  But I don't want to.

C

Being without you

  Em7

Is all a big mistake,

  F

In-stead of getting easier,

     Fm6

It's the hardest thing to take.

    F   G

I'm ad-dicted to you, babe,

      Ab Bb   C

You're a hard habit to break.

Verse 2

    F#
You found someone else, you had every reason,

D#m7
  You know I can't blame you for runnin' to him.

    B   A#m7   D#m7
Two people together but livin' alone,

   G#m7   E
I was spreading my love too thin.

F#m7 E   A
Af - ter   all of these years

                   F#m7
I'm still try'n to shake it,

Doin' much better.

(They say that it just takes time.)

   D
But deep in the night,

    C#m7   F#m7
It's an endless fight,

 Bm7   G Am7 G
I can't get you out of my mind.

Chorus 2

     C
Now being without you

     Em
Takes a lot of getting used to,

F
  Should learn to live with it

Fm6
  But I don't want to.

C
Being without you

  Em7
Is all a big mistake,

   F
In-stead of getting easier,

Fm6
It's the hardest thing to take.

    F   **G**
I'm ad-dicted to you, babe,

    A♭ B♭   **A♭maj7 Gm7 Cm7 Fm7 G7sus G7**
You're a hard habit to break.

Verse 2

E♭   **B♭**
    Can't go on,

E♭   **A♭ G7sus G7**
Just can't go on,   on.

E♭   **B♭**
    Can't go on,

E♭   **A♭ G7sus G7**
Just can't go on,   on.

| **Am7** | **Fm** | **E♭** | **E♭m** | **F** | | **E♭m** | **F7sus** | **C** | **B** | |

Chorus 3

    C
Now being without you

    Em
Takes a lot of getting used to,

F
   Should learn to live with it

Fm6
   But I don't want to.

C
Being without you

   Em7
Is all a big mistake,

   F
In-stead of getting easier,

    Fm6
It's the hardest thing to take.

    F   **G**
I'm ad-dicted to you, babe.

    A♭ B♭   **A♭ B♭**
‖: You're a hard habit to break.   :‖   *Repeat and fade*

Heart and Soul

Words and Music by Mike Chapman
and Nicky Chinn

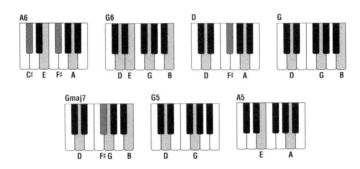

| *Intro* | ‖: A6 | G6 | :‖ | *Play 3 times* |
| | D | | | |

Verse 1
A6   G6
Two o'clock this morn - ing

A6   G6
If she should come a call - ing

A6   G6   G Gmaj7
I wouldn't dream of turn-ing her away.

Verse 2
A6   G6
And if it got hot and hec - tic

A6   G6
I know she'd be elec - tric.

A6   G6   G Gmaj7
I'd let her take her chan - ces with me.

She gets what she wants

Copyright © 1981 by Universal Music - MGB Songs
International Copyright Secured   All Rights Reserved

Chorus 1

```
G                                    A5
    'Cause she's heart and soul.

G5                      A5
    She's hot and cold.

G5                 A5
    She's got it all.

                A6     G6
Hot loving ev'ry night.

        A6  G6
Whoa.

        A6  G6  D
Whoa.
```

Verse 3

```
A6                              G6
    Well, can't you see her standing__ there?

A6                              G6
    See how she looks, see how she__ cares.

A6                     G6              G   Gmaj7
    I let her steal the night    away from me.
```

Verse 4

```
A6                      G6
    Nine o'clock this morn - ing

A6                      G6
    She left without a warn - ing.

A6                      G6         G   Gmaj7
    I let her take advantage__ of me.
```

She got what she wanted

Chorus 2   **Repeat Chorus 1**

Chorus 3
G   A5
　　　Yeah, she's heart and soul.

G5   A5
　　She's hot and cold.

G5   A5
　　She's got it all.

G5   A5   G5
　　She's heart and soul.

Yeah.

Solo   **Repeat Chorus 1 (Instrumental)**

Outro
                        A6   G6
She's got loving ev'ry night.

            A6   G6
Whoa.

            A6   G6
Whoa.

                    A6   G6
She's got it all.

                        A6   G6
‖: She's heart and soul.   :‖   **Repeat and fade**

How to Save a Life

Words and Music by Joseph King
and Isaac Slade

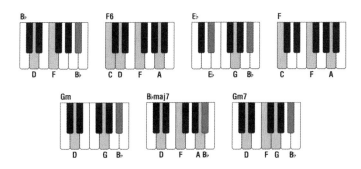

Intro

| Bb | F6/A | Bb | F6/A | |

Verse 1

          Bb   **F6/A**
Step one, ____ you say we need ____ to talk.

         Bb   **F6/A**   **Bb**
He walks, ____ you say, "Sit down, ____ it's just a talk."

        F6/A
He smiles polite - ly back at you.

Bb   **F6/A**
  You stare polite - ly right on through

Bb   **F6/A**   **Bb**
  Some sort of win - dow to your right,

       F6/ A   **Bb**
As he goes left ____ and you stay right.

        F6/A   **Bb**
Between the lines ____ of fear and blame,

        F6/A
You begin to won - der why you came.

© 2005 EMI APRIL MUSIC INC. and AARON EDWARDS PUBLISHING
All Rights Controlled and Administered by EMI APRIL MUSIC INC.
All Rights Reserved   International Copyright Secured   Used by Permission

Chorus 1

Eb   F
Where did I go wrong?

   Gm   Bbmaj7   F/A
I lost a friend ____ somewhere along ____ in the bit - terness.

  Eb   F   Gm
And I would have stayed up ____ with you all night

    Bbmaj7 F/A Bb F6/A Bb F6/A
Had I known how to save ____ a life.

Verse 2

Bb   F6/A
Let him know that you ____ know best

  Gm7   F6/A
'Cause after all you do ____ know best.

Bb   F6/A
 Try to slip past his ____ defense

Gm7   F6/A
Without granting in - nocence.

Bb   F6/A   Gm7
 Lay down a list ____ of what is wrong,

      F6/A
The things you've told ____ him all along.

Bb   F6/A
Pray to God he hears ____ you,

  Gm7   F6/A
And I pray to God he hears ____ you.

And…

Chorus 2   *Repeat Chorus 1*

Verse 3

        Bb   F6/A
As he begins to raise ____ his voice,

        Gm7   F6/A   Bb
You lower yours and grant him one last choice.

                  F6/A
Drive until you lose ____ the road,

        Gm7   F6/A
Or break with the ones you've fol - lowed.

        Bb   F6/A
He will do one ____ of two things,

        Gm7   F6/A
He will admit to ev - 'rything,

        Bb   F6/A
Or he'll say he's just not the same

        Gm7   F6/A
And you'll begin to won - der why you came.

Chorus 3

        Eb   F
‖: Where did I go wrong?

            Gm   Bbmaj7   F/A
I lost a friend ____ somewhere along ____ in the bit - terness.

        Eb   F   Gm
And I would have stayed up ____ with you all night

            Bbmaj7   F/A   Bb F6/A Bb
Had I known how to save ____ a life. :‖

Eb/A   Bb F6/A Bb F6/A
How to save a life.   How to save a life.

Outro/Chorus

        Eb   F
‖: Where did I go wrong?

            Gm   Bbmaj7   F/A
I lost a friend ____ somewhere along ____ in the bit - terness.

        Eb   F   Gm
And I would have stayed up ____ with you all night

            Bbmaj7   F/A   Bb F6/A Bb
Had I known how to save ____ a life. :‖

F6/A   Bb F6/A Bb
How to save a life.

F6/A   Bb F6/A Bb F6/A Bb
How to save a life.

Heartache Tonight

Words and Music by John David Souther,
Don Henley, Glenn Frey and Bob Seger

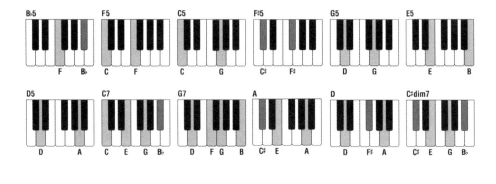

Intro |B♭5 F5 C5 F♯5 |G5 | | |

G5

Verse 1   Somebody's gonna hurt someone

Before the night is through.

Somebody's gonna come undone,

There's nothin' we can do.

       E5
Ev'rybody wants to touch somebody,

G5   **E5**
 If it takes all night.

G5   **C5**
 Ev'rybody wants to take a little chance,

G5   **D5**
 Make it come out right.

© 1979 EMI BLACKWOOD MUSIC INC., WOODY CREEK MUSIC, RED CLOUD MUSIC and GEAR PUBLISHING CO.
All Rights Reserved   International Copyright Secured   Used by Permission

Chorus 1

            C7
There's gonna be a heartache tonight,

                  G7
A heartache tonight, I know.

            C7
There's gonna be a heartache tonight,

                 A
A heartache tonight, I know.

   D
Lord, I know.

Verse 2

G5   **E5**
   Some people like to stay out late.

G5   **E5**
Some folks can't hold out that long.

   G5   **C5**
But nobody wants to go home now;

G5   **D5**
   There's too much goin' on.

G5   **E5**
   This night is gonna last forever.

G5   **E5**
Last all, last all summer long.

G5   **C5**
   Some time before the sun comes up

G5   **D5**
   The radio is gonna play that song.

Chorus 2
C7
There's gonna be a heartache tonight,

G7
A heartache tonight, I know.

C7
There's gonna be a heartache tonight,

A
A heartache tonight, I know.

D
Lord, I know.

G5
There's gonna be a heartache tonight,

The moon's shinin' bright,

C7
So turn out the light,

C#dim7
And we'll get it right.

G5
There's gonna be a heartache tonight,

D5   G5
A heartache tonight, I know.

| B♭5 F5   C5 F#5 | G5 |

| B♭5 F5   C5 F#5 | G5 | |

Verse 3   *Repeat Verse 1*

Chorus 3   ***Repeat Chorus 1***

G5

Outro   We can beat around the bushes,

We can get down to the bone,

C7
We can leave it in the parking lot,

C#dim7
But either way,

G5
There's gonna be a heartache tonight,

D5   **G5**
A heartache tonight, I know.

C7
Oh, I know.

G5
There'll be a heart - ache tonight,

D5   **G5**
A heartache tonight, I know.

‖: Bb5 F5 C5 F#5 │G5   :‖   *Play 3 times*

│ Bb5 F5 C5 F#5 │G5   │   │

Heroes

Words by David Bowie
Music by David Bowie and Brian Eno

Intro   ‖: D |G | | :‖

                D   **G**

Verse 1   I,__ I will be king.

                       D   **G**

         And you,__ you will be queen.

                     C

         Though nothing

                                D

         Will drive them away,

                 Am   **Em**

         We can beat them

                       D

         Just for one day.

                     C   **G**

         We can be he - roes

                       D

         Just for one day.

                D

Verse 2   And you,

                     G

         You can be mean.

             D

         And I,

                   G

         I'll drink all the time.

© 1977 (Renewed 2005) EMI MUSIC PUBLISHING LTD., TINTORETTO MUSIC and UNIVERSAL MUSIC PUBLISHING MGB LTD.
All Rights for EMI MUSIC PUBLISHING LTD. Controlled and Administered by SCREEN GEMS-EMI MUSIC INC.
All Rights for TINTORETTO MUSIC Administered by RZO MUSIC
All Rights for UNIVERSAL MUSIC PUBLISHING MGB LTD. in the U.S. Administered by UNIVERSAL MUSIC - CAREERS
All Rights Reserved   International Copyright Secured   Used by Permission

     D
'Cause we're lov - ers,

      G
And that is a fact.

     D
Yes, we're lov - ers,

      G
And that is that.

    C
Though nothing

      D
Will keep us togeth - er,

        Am **Em**
We could steal time

      D
Just for one day.

     C   **G**
We can be he - roes

      D
Forever and ev - er.

What'd you say?

Interlude 1 **Repeat Intro**

     D   **G**
Verse 3 I, I wish you could swim

      D
Like the dol - phins,

          G
Like the dolphins can swim.

     C
Though nothing,

         D
Nothing will keep us togeth - er,

    Am   **Em**
We can beat them

      D
Forever and ev - er.

          C   **G**
Oh, we can be he - roes

              D
Just for one day.

Interlude 2 Repeat Intro

    D   **G**
Verse 4   I, I will be king.

        D   **G**
And you,__ you will be queen.

        C
Though nothing

             D
Will drive them away,

         Am   **Em**
We can be he-roes

          D
Just for one day.

        C   **G**
We can be us

          D
Just for one day.

    D   **G**
Verse 5   I, I can remem - ber

    D   **G**
Standing by the wall.

      D
The guns

        G
Shot above our heads,

        D
And we kissed

            G
As though nothing could fall.

     C
And the shame

        D
Was on the other side.

            Am   **Em**
Oh, we can beat__ them

        D
Forever and ever.

             C   **G**
Then we could be heroes

         D
Just for one day.

What'd you say?

Interlude 3   **Repeat Intro**

        D   **G**
Verse 6   We can be heroes

        D
Just for one__ day.

             G
We can be heroes.

      C
We're nothing,

            D
And nothing will help__ us.

        Am   **Em**
Maybe we're lying;

           D
Then you better not stay.

         C   **G**
But we could be saf - er

         D
Just for one day.

Outro   **Repeat Intro till fade**

I Will Remember You

Theme from THE BROTHERS McMULLEN

Words and Music by Sarah McLachlan,
Seamus Egan and Dave Merenda

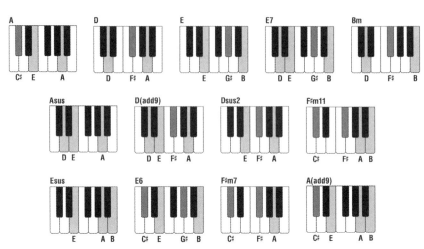

Chorus 1	A D E	

Chorus 1

      A   D   E
I will re-member you.

      A   D   E E7
Will you re-member me?

         A   D   A   Bm
Don't let your life__   pass you by.

      A   E7   A
Weep not for the memories.

Verse 1

        A   D(add9)   E   E7
   I'm so__ tired but I can't sleep.

      A   Dsus2   E   F♯m11
Standin' on the edge__ of somethin' much too deep.

        A   Dsus2   E
It's funny how we feel__ so much but cannot say a word.

               A   D(add9) Esus
Though we are screamin' inside,__ oh,   we can't be heard.

Copyright © 1995 Sony/ATV Music Publishing LLC, Tyde Music, Seamus Egan Music and T C F Music Publishing, Inc.
All Rights on behalf of Sony/ATV Music Publishing LLC and Tyde Music Administered by Sony/ATV Music Publishing LLC,
8 Music Square West, Nashville, TN 37203
All Rights on behalf of Seamus Egan Music Administered by Fox Film Music Corp.
International Copyright Secured   All Rights Reserved

Chorus 2

A   Dsus2   A
I will re-member you.__ (De, de, da, da, da.)

       Dsus2   E   E7 E6
Will you re-member me?__ (Do, de, da, da.)

E A   Dsus2   A   Bm
Don't let your life__   pass you by.

A   Dsus2   E7   A
Weep not for__   the memories.

Solo

A	Dsus2	E		
A	Dsus2	E	F#m11	
A	Dsus2	E		
A	D(add9)	Esus		

Verse 2

    A   Asus   E7
I'm so afraid to love you, but more afraid to lose.

A   Asus   E7   F#m
Clinging to a past that doesn't let me choose.

    A   Dsus2   E
But once there was a dark - ness, a deep and endless night.

    A   D(add9)   Esus
You gave me ev'rything__ you had, oh,__ you gave me light.

Chorus 3   **Repeat Chorus 2**

Chorus 4

A   Dsus2   A
I will re-member you.__ (De, de, da, da, da.)

       Dsus2   E   E7 E6
Will you re-member me?__ (Do, de, da, da.)

E A   Dsus2   A   Bm
Don't let your life__   pass you by.

(Do, de, da, da, da.)

A   Dsus2   E7   A   A(add9)
Weep not for__   the memo - ries.

I'm the Only One

Words and Music by
Melissa Etheridge

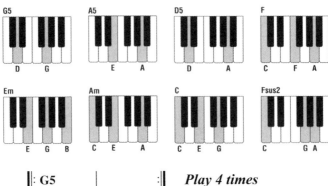

Intro ‖: G5 | :‖ *Play 4 times*

Verse 1
G5
Please, baby, can't you see my mind's a burnin' hell?

I got razors a rippin' and tearin' and

Strippin' my heart apart as well.

Tonight you told me that you ache for somethin' new,

'Cause some other woman is lookin'

Like somethin' that might be good for you.

Pre-Chorus 1
A5
Go on and hold her

D5
'Til the screamin' is gone.

A5
Go on, believe her

D5
When she tells you nothin's wrong.

Copyright © 1993 MLF Music (ASCAP)
All Rights Reserved   Used by Permission

Chorus 1

G5
   But I'm the only one

     F   Em
Who'll walk across a fire for you.

G5
   And I'm the only one

     F   Em
Who'll drown in my desire for you.

     Am
It's only fear that makes you run,

     C
The demons that you're hidin' from

     Fsus2   C
When all your promises are gone.

     G5
I'm the only__ one.

Verse 2

G5
Please, baby, can't you see I'm tryin' to explain

I've been here before and I'm lockin' the door

And I'm not goin' back again.

Her eyes and arms and skin won't make it go away.

You'll wake up tomorrow and wrestle the sorrow

That holds you down today.

Pre-Chorus 2   **Repeat Pre-Chorus 1**

Chorus 2   **Repeat Chorus 1**

Solo   ‖: **Fsus2** | | **G5** | :‖

Pre-Chorus 3   **Repeat Pre-Chorus 1**

Chorus 3

G5
But I'm the only one

F   Em
Who'll walk across a fire for you.

G5
And I'm the only one

F   Em
Who'll drown in my desire for you.

Am
It's only fear that makes you run,

C
The demons that you're hidin' from

Fsus2   C
When all your promises are gone.

G5
I'm the only__ one.

F   Em
Yeah,   yeah.

G5
And I'm the only one

F   Em
Who'll drown in my desire for you.

Am
It's only fear that makes you run,

C
The demons that you're hiding from

Fsus2   C
When all your promises are gone.

G5
I'm the on - ly one.

I'm the only one, babe.

I'm the only one.

Ain't nobody else is gonna love you,

Ain't nobody else is gonna love you.   *(Fade out)*

If I Ever Lose My Faith in You

Music and Lyrics by
Sting

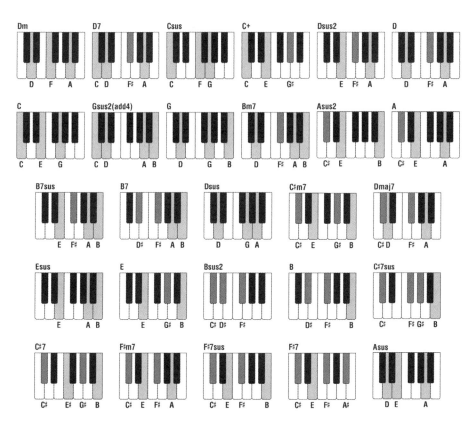

Intro | Dm | | D7 | | |
       | Csus | | C+ | | |

          Dsus2   D
Verse 1   You could say I

       C   Gsus2(add4)   G   Gsus2(add4) G
       Lost my faith in sci-ence   and progress.

© 1992 STEERPIKE LTD.
Administered by EMI MUSIC PUBLISHING LIMITED
All Rights Reserved   International Copyright Secured   Used by Permission

Dsus2   D
You could say I

          C   Gsus2(add4) G Gsus2(add4) G
Lost my be-lief in the holy church.

Dsus2   D
You could say I

C   Gsus2(add4) G Gsus2(add4) G
Lost my sense of direc-tion.

Dsus2 D   Bm7
          You could say all of this and worse, but

Chorus 1
Asus2 A   B7sus   B7   C   Dsus D
          If I ever lose__ my faith__ in you

Asus2   A   B7sus   B7   C   Dsus D
          There'd be nothing left__ for me__ to do.

Verse 2
Dsus2   D
          Some would say I was a

C   Gsus2(add4) G Gsus2(add4) G
Lost man in a lost world.

Dsus2   D
You could say I

C   Gsus2(add4) G Gsus2(add4) G
Lost my faith in the people on TV.

Dsus2   D
You could say I

          C   Gsus2(add4) G Gsus2(add4) G
Lost my be-lief in our poli-ticians.

Dsus2 D   Bm7
          They all seem like game show hosts to me.

Chorus 2   ***Repeat Chorus 1***

Interlude |C   A |C   A |C   A |C   A |

Bridge
Bm7   C#m7   Dmaj7   Esus E
          I could be lost inside their lies   with-out a trace.

Bsus2 B   C#7sus C#7   E   D   E   D
          But every time I   close my eyes   I see your face.

Verse 3

Dsus2 D
       I never saw no

C   Gsus2(add4) G Gsus2(add4) G
   Miracle of sci-ence

Dsus2 D
   That didn't go

          C   Gsus2(add4) G Gsus2(add4) G
From a   blessing to a curse.

Dsus2 D
       I never saw no

C   Gsus2(add4) G Gsus2(add4) G
   Military solution

Dsus2 D   Bm7
       That didn't always end up as something worse,

  Asus2   A   F#m7
But   let me say this first.

Chorus 3

Esus E   F#7sus   F#7   G
   If I ever lose__ my faith__ in you,

          Asus   A
If I ever lose__ my faith__ in you,

Esus   E   F#7sus   F#7
   There'd be nothing left__ for me__ to do.

G   Asus   A
   There'd be nothing left__ for me__ to do.

Asus2 A   B7sus   B7
   If I ever lose__ my faith,

C   Dsus   D
   If I ever lose__ my faith,

Asus2 A   B7sus   B7
   If I ever lose__ my faith,

C   Dsus   D Dsus D
   If I ever lose__ my faith__   in you…

Outro   ‖: C   A | C   A   :‖   *Repeat and fade*

If It Makes You Happy

Words and Music by Jeff Trott
and Sheryl Crow

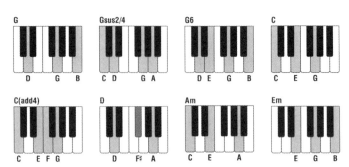

Intro	|G Gsus2/4| G G6 G | Gsus2/4| G G6 G |

\|G Gsus2/4\| G G6 G \| Gsus2/4\|

Verse 1

Gsus2/4 G G6 G   Gsus2/4   G   Gsus2/4 G
                I   be - long ___ a long way from here.

G   Gsus2/4
Put on a poncho, ___ played for mosquitoes

G   C Cadd4 C   Cadd4
And drank till I was thirsty again.

C   G   Gsus2/4   G   Gsus2/4
  We were search - in'   through thrift store jun - gles.

      G   Gsus2/4
Found Ge - ronimo's rifle,   Marilyn's shampoo,

G   C
And Benny Goodman's corset and pen.

Pre-Chorus 1

    C   D
  Well, okay, I made this up.

    C   D
I promised you I'd never give up.

Copyright © 2001 by Trottsky Music, Warner-Tamerlane Publishing Corp. and Old Crow Music
All Rights for Trottsky Music Administered by Kobalt Music Publishing America, Inc.
All Rights Reserved Used by Permission

Chorus 1

    N.C.   Am   C   G
If it makes you hap - py,   it can't be that bad.

    D   Am
    If it makes you hap - py,

    C   G   Gsus2/4 G G6 G
    Then why the hell are you so ___ sad?

  |G   Gsus2/4|

Verse 2

    Gsus2/4 G   G6 G   Gsus2/4 G   Gsus2/4
           You get down, ___ a real low ___ down.

    G   Gsus2/4
    You listen to Coltrane,   derail your own train.

    G   C Cadd4 C   Cadd4
    Well, who hasn't been there before?

    C   G   Gsus2/4   G   Gsus2/4
    I come 'round,   around the hard ___ way.

        G   Gsus2/4
    Bring you comics in bed, scrape the mold off the bread

    G   C
    And serve you French toast again.

Pre-Chorus 2

    C   D
    Well, okay, I still get stoned.

        C   D
    I'm not the kind of girl you take home.

Chorus 2

    N.C.   Am
    If it makes you hap - py,

    C   G
    It can't be that bad.

    D   Am
    If it makes you hap - py,

    C   G   Gsus2/4 G Gsus2/4 G
    Then why the hell are you so ___ sad?

Chorus 3

Gsus2/4   G   Gsus2/4   D   Am
If it makes _____ you _____ hap - py,

C   G
It can't be that bad.

D   Am
If it makes you hap - py,

C   Em   Am
Then why the hell are you so ____ sad?

| Em | | C | | |

Interlude

| G   Gsus2/4 | G   G6   G | G   Gsus2/4 |

Verse 3

Gsus2/4   G   G6   G   Gsus2/4   G   Gsus2/4
           We've been far, ____   far away from here.

G   Gsus2/4
   Put on a poncho, ____ played for mosquitoes

G   C
And ev'rywhere in between.

Pre-Chorus 3

C   D
   Well, okay, we get along.

C   D
So what if right now ev'rything's wrong?

Chorus 4   *Repeat Chorus 2*

Chorus 5

Gsus2/4   G   Gsus2/4   D   Am
If it makes _____ you _____ hap - py,

C   G
It can't be that bad.

D   Am
If it makes you hap - py,

C   G   Gsus2/4   G   Gsus2/4   G
Then why the hell are you so ____ sad?

| Gsus2/4   G   Gsus2/4   D |

Guitar Solo

| Am | C | G | |
| D | Am | C | |
Oh,   oh.

Outro

|: G   Gsus2/4 | G :| *Play 3 times*
| G | |

Iris

from the Motion Picture CITY OF ANGELS

Words and Music by
John Rzeznik

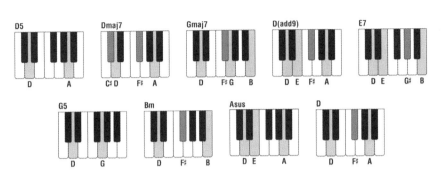

Intro   ‖: D5 Dmaj7/C♯ D5 │ Gmaj7 D(add9)/F♯ D5   :‖

Verse 1

          D5   **E7**   **G5**
And I'd give up forev - er to touch__ you

             Bm   **Asus**   **G5**
'Cause I know__ that you feel__ me some-how.

            D5   **E7**   **G5**
You're the clos - est to heav - en that I'll__ ever be,

          Bm   **Asus**   **G5**
And I don't__ wanna go__ home right now.

        D5   **E7**   **G5**
And all__ I could taste__ is this moment,

         Bm   **Asus**   **G5**
And all__ I can breathe__ is your life.

       D5   **E7**   **G5**
Well, sooner or lat - er it's o - ver.

         Bm   **Asus**   **G5**
I just don't__ wanna miss__ you tonight.

© 1998 EMI VIRGIN SONGS, INC. and SCRAP METAL MUSIC
All Rights Controlled and Administered by EMI VIRGIN SONGS, INC.
All Rights Reserved   International Copyright Secured   Used by Permission

Chorus 1

       Bm   Asus   G5
And I don't want the world__ to see__ me

          Bm   Asus   G5
'Cause I don't__ think that they'd__ under-stand.

      Bm   Asus   G5
When everything's made to be bro - ken

        Bm   Asus   G5
I just want__ you to know__ who I am.

Interlude 1   **Repeat Intro**

Verse 2

        D5   E7   G5
And you can't__ fight the tears__ that ain't comin',

      Bm   Asus   G5
Or the mo - ment of truth__ in your lies.

      D5   E7   G5
When ev'rything feels like the mov - ies,

        Bm   Asus   G5
Yeah, you bleed__ just to know__ you're alive.

Chorus 2   **Repeat Chorus 1**

Interlude 2   ‖:Bm Dmaj7/C♯ |D5 |Bm   Asus |G5   :‖
                   ‖:Bm Dmaj7/C♯   D5 |G5   :‖   *Play 4 times*
                   |D/F♯ |G5 |Bm |G5 |
                   |D/F♯ |Bm |
                   | Dmaj7/C♯ D5 E7 D5 Dmaj7/C♯ |
                   |G5 |D/F♯ |Bm | |
                   ‖:Bm Dmaj7/C♯ |D5 |Bm   Asus |G5   :‖

Chorus 3   **Repeat Chorus 1**

Chorus 4   **Repeat Chorus 1**

                              Bm   Asus   G5
Outro   I just want__ you to know__ who I am.

                              Bm   Asus   G5
                   I just want__ you to know__ who I am.

                              Bm   Asus   G5
                   I just want__ you to know__ who I am.

                              Bm   Asus   Bm
                   I just want__ you to know__ who I am.
                   ‖: Bm Dmaj7/C♯ |D5 |Bm Asus |G5 :‖ *Repeat and fade*

If You Leave Me Now

Words and Music by
Peter Cetera

If you leave me now, __

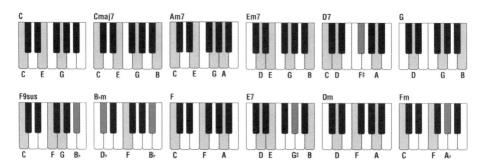

Intro | C G C   G C | G   C |
           | C G C   G C | |

Verse 1
               Cmaj7
If you leave me now,

              Am7   **Em7**
You'll take away the biggest part__ of me.

            Am7 **D7**   **G**   **C G C**
Ooh,__ no,__ baby please__ don't go.

Verse 2
               Cmaj7
And if you leave me now,

              Am7   **Em7**
You'll take away the very heart__ of me.

            Am7 **D7**   **G**   **C G C**
Ooh,__ no,__ baby please__ don't go.

            Am7 **D7** **G**   **C G C**
Ooh__ girl,__ I just want you to stay.

Copyright © 1976 by Universal Music - MGB Songs and Big Elk Music
Copyright Renewed
International Copyright Secured   All Rights Reserved

Chorus 1

F9sus   B♭m   F
  A love like ours is love__ that's hard to find.

Am7   F   G   C Am7 E7
  How could we let__ it slip__ away?

F9sus   B♭m   F
  We've come too far to leave__ it all behind.

Am7   F   G   C
  How could we end__ it all__ this way?

    Em7
When tomor - row comes,

     Am7   Dm   Em7   Fm
Then we'll both regret the things we said to - day.

Solo   ***Repeat Verse 1 (Instrumental)***

Chorus 2 ***Repeat Chorus 1 till fade***

Imagine

Words and Music by
John Lennon

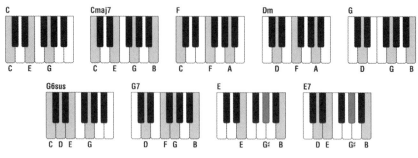

Intro ‖: C   Cmaj7 | F   :‖

Verse 1

C   Cmaj7   F
  Imagine there's no heaven.

C   Cmaj7   F
  It's easy if you__ try.

C   Cmaj7   F
  No hell below us,

C   Cmaj7   F
  Above us only sky.

Pre-Chorus 1

F   C   Dm
  Imagine all__ the peo-ple

G   G6sus G7
Living for today.

Verse 2

C   Cmaj7   F
  Imagine there's no countries.

C   Cmaj7 F
  It isn't hard to do.

C   Cmaj7   F
  Nothing to kill or die__ for

C   Cmaj7   F
  And no religion,__ too.

© 1971 (Renewed 1999) LENONO.MUSIC
All Rights Controlled and Administered by EMI BLACKWOOD MUSIC INC.
All Rights Reserved   International Copyright Secured   Used by Permission

Pre-Chorus 2

       F   C   Dm
Imagine all__ the peo-ple

G   G6sus   G7
Living life in peace.

Chorus 1

           F   G   C   Cmaj7 E E7
You,__you may say I'm a dreamer.

F   G   C Cmaj7 E E7
But I'm not the only one.

F   G   C   Cmaj7 E E7
I hope some day you'll join us

F   G   C
And the world will be as one.

Verse 3

C   Cmaj7   F
Imagine no possessions.

C   Cmaj7   F
I wonder if you__ can.

C   Cmaj7 F
No need for greed or hunger,

C   Cmaj7   F
A brotherhood of__ man.

Pre-Chorus 3

F   C   Dm
Imagine all__ the peo-ple

G   G6sus   G7
Sharing all the world.

Chorus 2

           F   G   C   Cmaj7 E E7
You,__ you may say I'm a dreamer.

F   G   C Cmaj7 E E7
But I'm not the only one.

F   G   C   Cmaj7 E E7
I hope some day you'll join us

F   G   C
And the world will live as one.

Jack and Diane

Words and Music by
John Mellencamp

  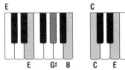

Intro   ‖: A | E   A E | D N.C. | D | N.C. :‖   *Play 3 times*

Verse 1

    A   E   D   E
       A little ditty about Jack and Di-ane,

    A   E   D   E   A
       Two Ameri-can kids growin' up in the heart-land.

                E   D   E
Jack, he's gonna be a football star.

    A   E   D   E   A
       Diane's debutante back seat of Jack - y's car.

| A   E | D   E | A   E | D   A |

Verse 2

    A   E   D   E
       Suckin' on a chili dog out-side the Tastee Freez;

    A   E
       Diane sittin' on Jacky's lap.

             D   E   A
He's got his hands be-tween her knees.

                E
Jack, he says, "Hey, Diane,

             D   E
Let's run off be-hind a shady tree;

    A   E
       Dribble off those Bobbie Brooks.

       D   E   A
Let me do what__ I please."

© 1982 EMI FULL KEEL MUSIC
All Rights Reserved   International Copyright Secured   Used by Permission

	A E D E
Chorus 1	Sayin', oh yeah, life goes on,

       A   E   D   E
Long after the thrill of living is gone.

          A   E   D   E
Sayin',   oh yeah, life goes on,

         A   E   D E A
Long after the thrill of living is gone. Now, walk on.

Interlude   ‖: A | E   A E | D N.C. | D N.C. :‖

        A   E
Verse 3   Jack, he sits back,

           D   E
Collects his thoughts for a moment;

      A   E
      Scratches his head and does his

D E   A
Best James Dean.

           E
 "Well, then, there, Diane,

          D   E
We gotta run off to the city."

     A   E
     Diane says, "Baby,

         D   E A
You ain't missin'__ a thing."

But Jack, he says...

Chorus 2   ***Repeat Chorus 1***

Bridge   N.C.
Oh, let it rock, let it roll.

Let the Bible Belt come and save my soul.

Holdin' on to sixteen as long as you can;

Change is comin' 'round real soon,

Make us women and men.

Interlude | C   E | D   E | A   E | D   A |

Chorus 3   **Repeat Chorus 1**

Outro   A   E   D   E
A little ditty about Jack and Di-ane,

A   E
Two Ameri-can kids doin'

    D   E   A
The best that they can.

‖: A   E | A   E   A   E | D   N.C. | D   N.C. :‖ *Repeat and fade*

Learning to Fly

Words and Music by Tom Petty
and Jeff Lynne

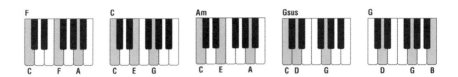

F   C   Am   Gsus   G

Intro   ‖: F   C | Am   Gsus4   :‖   *Play 4 times*

         F   **C**   **Am**   **Gsus4**
Verse 1   Well, I started out

         F   **C**   **Am**   **Gsus4**
Down a dirty road,

F   **C**   **Am**   **Gsus4**
Started out

F   **C**   **Am**   **Gsus4**
All a-lone.

         F   **C**   **Am**   **Gsus4**
Verse 2   And the sun went down

         F   **C**   **Am**   **Gsus4**
As I crossed the hill

         F   **C**   **Am**   **Gsus4**
And the town lit up,

     F   **C**   **Am**   **Gsus4**
The world got still.

Copyright © 1991 Gone Gator Music and EMI April Music Inc.
All Rights Reserved   Used by Permission

Chorus 1
```
      F        C    Am   G
```
I'm learning to fly,

```
       F      C       Am   G
```
But I ain't got wings.

```
 F      C      Am     G
```
Comin' down

```
       F      C          Am   G
```
Is the hardest thing.

Verse 3
```
        F       C      Am    Gsus4
```
Well, the good old days

```
      F     C       Am      Gsus4
```
May not re-turn,

```
      F          C       Am     Gsus4
```
And the rocks might melt,

```
      F         C       Am     Gsus4
```
And the sea may burn.

Chorus 2   **Repeat Chorus 1**

Solo   ‖: F   C   │Am   G   :‖   *Play 4 times*

Verse 4
```
      F       C     Am   Gsus4
```
Well, some say life

```
      F     C      Am    Gsus4
```
Will beat you down,

```
     F        C      Am   Gsus4
```
An' break your heart,

```
      F        C      Am    Gsus4
```
And steal your crown.

Verse 5
```
      F    C    Am    Gsus4
```
So I started out

```
      F        C      Am    Gsus4
```
For God knows where,

```
                 F       C       Am      Gsus4
              I guess I'll know

                      F    C      Am      Gsus4
              When I get there.


                      F         C    Am    G
Chorus 3      I'm learning to fly

                      F         C         Am    G
              A-round the clouds.

              F         C    Am    G
              What goes up

              F         C         Am    G
              Must come down.


Interlude     ‖: F     C      │ Am      G          :‖


                      F         C
Chorus 4      ‖: I'm learning to fly,

              Am        G
              (Learning to fly.)

                      F    C      Am    G
              But I ain't got wings.

              F    C      Am    G
              Coming down

                      F    C      Am    G
              Is the hardest thing.

                      F         C
              I'm learning to fly

              Am        G
              (Learning to fly.)

                      F    C      Am    G
              A-round the clouds.

                      F    C      Am    G
              An' what goes up

              F         C      Am    G
              Must come down.              :‖    Repeat and fade
```

Kokomo

from the Motion Picture COCKTAIL

Words and Music by Mike Love,
Terry Melcher, John Phillips and Scott McKenzie

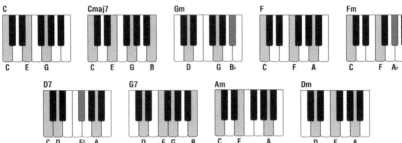

Intro

N.C.
(Aruba, Jamaica,

Ooh, I wanna take ya.

Bermuda, Bahama,

Come on, pretty mama.

Key Largo, Montego,

Baby, why don't we go, Jamaica?)

Verse 1

               C Cmaj7
Off the Florida Keys

Gm   **F**
   There's a place called Kokomo.

Fm   **C**
   That's where you wanna go

      D7   **G7**
To get a-way from it all.

C   **Cmaj7**
   Bodies in the sand,

Gm   **F**
   Tropical drink melting in your hand.

© 1988 Touchstone Pictures Music & Songs, Inc., Buena Vista Music Company, Clair Audient Publishing,
Daywin Music, Inc., Honest John Music and Phillips-Tucker Music
Administered 100% by Touchstone Pictures Music & Songs, Inc. and Buena Vista Music Company
All Rights Reserved   Used by Permission

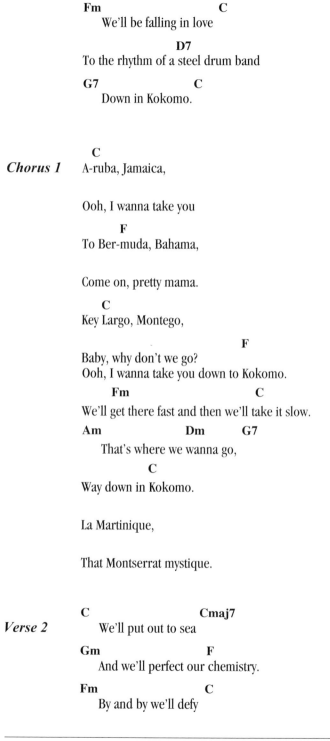

Fm   C
    We'll be falling in love

                    D7
To the rhythm of a steel drum band

G7   C
    Down in Kokomo.

                C
Chorus 1   A-ruba, Jamaica,

Ooh, I wanna take you

              F
To Ber-muda, Bahama,

Come on, pretty mama.

              C
Key Largo, Montego,

                            F
Baby, why don't we go?
Ooh, I wanna take you down to Kokomo.
          Fm   C
We'll get there fast and then we'll take it slow.
Am   Dm   G7
    That's where we wanna go,
                C
Way down in Kokomo.

La Martinique,

That Montserrat mystique.

C   Cmaj7
Verse 2   We'll put out to sea

Gm   F
    And we'll perfect our chemistry.

Fm   C
    By and by we'll defy

        D7   G7
A little bit of gravity.

C   **Cmaj7**
    Afternoon delight,

Gm   **F**
    Cocktails and moonlit nights.

Fm   **C**
    That dreamy look in your eye,

                    D7
Give me a tropical contact high

G7   **C**
    Way down in Kokomo.

              C
Chorus 2 A-ruba, Jamaica,

Ooh, I wanna take you

        F
To Ber-muda, Bahama,

Come on, pretty mama.

        C
Key Largo, Montego,

                              F
Baby, why don't we go?
Ooh, I wanna take you down to Kokomo.

        Fm   **C**
We'll get there fast and then we'll take it slow.

Am   **Dm**   **G7**
    That's where we wanna go,

                C
Way down in Kokomo.

Port Au Prince,

I wanna catch a glimpse.

Solo | C | Cmaj7 | Gm | F |
        | Fm | C | D7 | G7 |

Verse 3

C   Cmaj7
   Ev'rybody knows

Gm   F
   A little place like Kokomo.

Fm   C
   Now if you wanna go

          D7
And get a-way from it all,

G7   C
   Go down to Kokomo.

Chorus 3

      C
‖: A-ruba, Jamaica,

Ooh, I wanna take you

     F
To Ber-muda, Bahama,

Come on, pretty mama.

     C
Key Largo, Montego,

                   F
Baby, why don't we go?
Ooh, I wanna take you down to Kokomo.

    Fm   C
We'll get there fast and then we'll take it slow.

Am   Dm   G7
   That's where we wanna go,

      C
Way down in Kokomo.   :‖   ***Repeat and fade***

Let It Be

Words and Music by John Lennon
and Paul McCartney

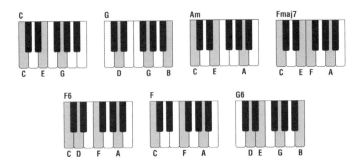

Verse 1

        C   **G**
When I find myself in times of trouble

Am   **Fmaj7**   **F6**
Mother Mary comes to me

C   **G**
Speaking words of wis - dom,

     F **C**
Let it be.

               G
And in my hour of dark - ness

     Am   **Fmaj7**   **F6**
She is standing right in front of me

C   **G**
Speaking words of wisdom,

     F **C**
Let it be.

Copyright © 1970 Sony/ATV Music Publishing LLC
Copyright Renewed
All Rights Administered by Sony/ATV Music Publishing LLC, 8 Music Square West, Nashville, TN 37203
International Copyright Secured   All Rights Reserved

                        Am   G6
Chorus 1   Let it be,__ let it be,

                        Fmaj7   **C**
              Ah, let it be,__ let it be.

                                    G
              Whisper words of wisdom,

                        F   C
              Let it be.

                        C   **G**
Verse 2   And when the broken heart - ed people

              Am   **Fmaj7**   **F6**
              Living in the world__ agree,

              C   **G**
              There will be an an - swer,

                        F   C
              Let it be.

                                            G
              For though they may be part-ed there is

              Am   **Fmaj7**   **F6**
              Still a chance that they__ will see

              C   **G**
              There will be an an-swer,

                        F   C
              Let it be.

                        Am   **G6**
Chorus 2   Let it be,__ let it be,

                        Fmaj7   **C**
              Ah, let it be,__ let it be.

                                    G
              Yeah, there will be an an - swer,

                        F   C
              Let it be.

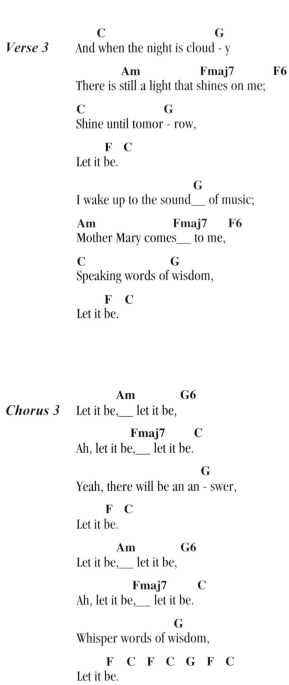

Verse 3

       C   **G**
And when the night is cloud - y

     Am   **Fmaj7**   **F6**
There is still a light that shines on me;

C   **G**
Shine until tomor - row,

     F   **C**
Let it be.

                     G
I wake up to the sound__ of music;

Am   **Fmaj7**   **F6**
Mother Mary comes__ to me,

C   **G**
Speaking words of wisdom,

     F   **C**
Let it be.

Chorus 3

     Am   **G6**
Let it be,__ let it be,

        Fmaj7   **C**
Ah, let it be,__ let it be.

              G
Yeah, there will be an an - swer,

     F   **C**
Let it be.

     Am   **G6**
Let it be,__ let it be,

        Fmaj7   **C**
Ah, let it be,__ let it be.

              G
Whisper words of wisdom,

     F   **C**   **F**   **C**   **G**   **F**   **C**
Let it be.

Listen to Your Heart

Words and Music by Per Gessle
and Mats Persson

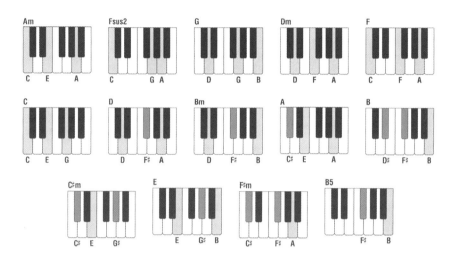

Intro

| Am Fsus2 | G Am | | Fsus2 | G Am |
| Fsus2 | G Am | | Fsus2 | Dm |

Verse 1

Am   Fsus2   G   Am
I know there's something in the wake of your smile.

    Fsus2   G   Am
I get a notion from the look in your eyes, yeah.

      Fsus2   G   Am
You've built a love but that love falls a - part.

                  Fsus2   Dm
Your little piece of heaven   turns to dark.

Copyright © 1989 Jimmy Fun Music
All Rights Administered by Sony/ATV Music Publishing LLC, 8 Music Square West, Nashville, TN 37203
International Copyright Secured   All Rights Reserved

Chorus 1

              Am **F**   **C**   **G**
Listen to your heart   when he's calling for you.

              Am **F**   **C**   **G**
Listen to your heart,   there's nothing else you can do.

       C   **G**   **F**   **C**
I don't know where you're going and I don't know why,

             Am
But listen to your heart

F   **G**   **Am** **Fsus2** **G** **Am**
  Before ___ you tell him good - bye.

| Am Fsus2 | G   Am |

Verse 2

Am   **Fsus2**   **G**   **Am**
  Sometimes you wonder if this fight is worth - while.

        Fsus2   **G**   **Am**
The pre - cious moments are all lost in the tide, yeah.

        Fsus2   **G**   **Am**
They're swept away and nothing is what it seems.

         Fsus2   **Dm**
The feeling of belonging   to your dreams.

Chorus 2

              Am **F**   **C**   **G**
Listen to your heart   when he's calling for you.

              Am **F**   **C**   **G**
Listen to your heart,   there's nothing else you can do.

       C   **G**   **F**   **C**
I don't know where you're going and I don't know why,

            Am **F**   **G**
But listen to your heart   before ___ you tell him goodbye.

Guitar Solo

| Am Fsus2 | G   Am | Fsus2 | G   Am |
| C   G | F   C | Am Fsus2 | G |

Bridge

D
And there are voices that want to be heard.

Bm
So much to mention but you can't find the words.

A   **G**
The scent of magic, the beauty that's been

A   **B**
When love was wilder   than the wind.

Chorus 3

             C#m A   **E**   **B**
‖: Listen to your heart   when he's calling for you.

            C#m A   **E**   **B**
Listen to your heart,   there's nothing else you can do.

      E   **B**   **A**   **E**
I don't know where you're going and I don't know why,

        C#m A   **B**
But listen to your heart   before... :‖

            C#m A B C#m
You tell him good - bye.

‖: **C#m**   **A** | **B**   **C#m** :‖
| **C#m**   **A** | **F#m** |

Outro

‖: **C#m**   **A** | **B**   **C#m** |
| **C#m B5 A** | **B**   **C#m** :‖   *Repeat and fade*
                                        w/ Vocal ad lib.

Looks Like We Made It

Words and Music by Richard Kerr
and Will Jennings

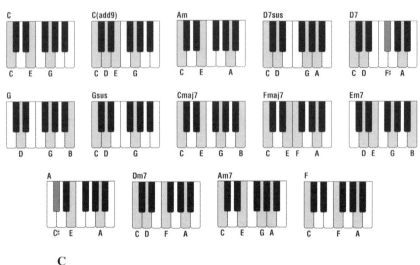

Verse 1

      C
      There you are,

F   **C(add9)**   **C**
Lookin' just the same as you did the last time I touched you.

Cadd9   **C**
      And here I am,

F   **C(add9)**   **C**
Close to gettin' tangled up inside the thought of you.

G   **Am**   **D7sus**   **D7**   **G**
      Do you love him as much as I__ love her?

    Am   **D7sus**   **D7**   **Gsus** **G**
And will that love be strong when old feelings start to stir?

Chorus 1

                C   **Cmaj7**
Looks like we made it.

         Fmaj7   **G**   **Em7** **A7** **Dm7**
Left each other on the way to another love.

Gsus   **C**   **Cmaj7**
      Looks like we made it,

Copyright © 1976 RONDOR MUSIC (LONDON) LTD. and IRVING MUSIC, INC.
Copyright Renewed
All Rights Reserved   Used by Permission

   Fmaj7   G   Em7   Am7
Or I thought so till today,__ until you were there, every-where,

    Dm7 C   F   G   C(add9) C G F
And all I could taste was love__ the way we made it.

    C
Verse 2   Love's so strange,

    F   C(add9) C
Playing hide and seek with hearts and always hurting.

    C(add9)   C
   And we're the fools,

    F   C(add9) C
Standing close enough to touch those burning memories.

     G Am   D7sus   D7   G
And if I hold you for the sake of all__ those times

      Am   D7sus
Love made us lose our minds,

      D7   Gsus G
Could I ever let you go?

Oh no, we've...

         C   Cmaj7
Chorus 2 Looks like we made it.

      Fmaj7   G   Em7 A7 Dm7
Left each other on the way to another love.

    Gsus   C   Cmaj7
   Looks like we made it,

     Fmaj7   G   Em7   Am7
Or I thought so till today,__ until you were there, every-where,

    Dm7 C   F   G   Am7
And all I could taste was love__ the way we made it.

    Em7 Am7   Gsus
Outro   Oh, we made it.

         C   Cmaj7 F
𝄆 Looks like we made it.   𝄇 *Repeat and fade*

Missing You

Words and Music by John Waite,
Charles Sanford and Mark Leonard

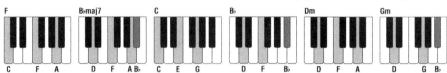

Intro

    F
Missing you,

Missing you.

B♭maj7
Missing you.

C
Missing you.

Verse 1

    F
Ev'ry time I think of you

    B♭   C
I always catch my breath.

          F
And I'm still standing here,

And you're miles away

    B♭   C
And I'm wond'rin' why you left.

         Dm
And there's a storm that's ragin'

       B♭   C
Through my frozen heart tonight.

        F
I hear your name in certain circles,

     B♭   C
And it always makes me smile.

        F
I spend my time thinkin' about you

Copyright © 1984 by Paperwaite Music, Fallwater Music and EverPop Songs, a div. of EverGreen Copyrights (admin. by ICG)
All Rights for Paperwaite Music Administered by Alley Music Corp. and Trio Music Company
All Rights for Fallwater Music Administered by WB Music Corp.
International Copyright Secured   All Rights Reserved
Used by Permission

        B♭   **C**
And it's almost drivin' me wild.

          Dm
And there's a heart that's breakin'

        B♭   **C**
Down this long distance line tonight.

              F
Chorus 1   I ain't missin' you at all

           B♭   **C**
Since you've been gone away.

          F
I ain't missin' you

        B♭maj7   **C**
No matter   what I might say.

          F
Verse 2   There's a message in the wire,

           B♭   **C**
And I'm sending you this signal tonight.

          F
You don't know

How desp'rate I've become,

     B♭   **C**
And it looks like I'm losin' this fight.

          F
In your world,__ I have no meaning.

      B♭   **C**
Though I'm tryin' hard to understand.

Dm
    And it's my heart that's breakin'

     B♭   **C**
Down__ this long distance line to-night.

             F
Chorus 2   I ain't missin' you at all

           B♭   **C**
Since you've been gone away.

                    F
I ain't missin' you

          B♭maj7   **C**
No matter   what my friends say.

Dm
     And there's a message that I'm sendin' out,

      B♭   **C**
Like__ a telegraph to your soul.

Dm
     And if I can't bridge this distance,

          B♭   **C**
Stop this   heartbreak over-load.

                              F
Chorus 3   I ain't missin' you at all

                    B♭   **C**
Since you've been gone away.

                    F
I ain't missin' you

          B♭maj7   **C**
No matter   what my friends say.

                F
I ain't miss-in' you.

                    B♭maj7
I ain't missin' you.

       C
I can lie to myself.

Dm
     And there's a storm that's ragin'

          B♭   **C**
Through__ my frozen heart to-night.

                    F
I ain't missin' you at all

                    B♭   **C**
Since you've been gone away.

                F
I ain't missin' you

          B♭maj7   **C**   **Gm F B♭ Gm F**
No matter   what my friends say.

More Than Words

Words and Music by Nuno Bettencourt
and Gary Cherone

Melody:

Say-ing "I ___ love ___ you"

    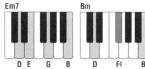

Intro   ‖: G G/B C(add9) | Am7 | C | D Dsus   G   :‖

                G G/B   C(add9)

Verse 1   Sayin', "I love you"

                Am7   C   D   Dsus G
                Is not the words I want to hear from   you.

                G/B   C(add9) Am7
                It's not that I want you   not to say,

                  C   D   Dsus   Em   Am7 D7
                But if you on - ly   knew how easy   it would be,

                  G   D/F#   Em
                To show me how you feel.

                      Am7   D7   G7 G7/B   C

Chorus 1   More than words is all you have to do to make it real.

                      Cm   G   Em
                Then you wouldn't have to say that you love me,

                  Am7   D7   G
                'Cause I'd al - ready know.

                      D/F#   Em   Bm   C
                What would you do__ if my heart was torn in two?

                          G/B Am7
                More than words to show you feel

Copyright © 1990 COLOR ME BLIND MUSIC
All Rights Administered by ALMO MUSIC CORP.
All Rights Reserved   Used by Permission

```
            D7              G
That your love for me is real.

                    D/F♯   Em      Bm     C
What would you say__ if I  took those words a-way?

                      G/B  Am7
Then you couldn't make things new

         D7                        G
Just by say - in', "I love you."
```

Interlude
```
       G  G/B  C(add9)                    Am7
                    La, dee, da , la, dee, da,

                  C
Dee, dai, dai, da.

D     Dsus G       G/B  C(add9)
More than   words.

                      Am7    D7
La, dee, da, dai, da.
```

Verse 2
```
       G  G/B          C(add9)  Am7
                    Now that I've tried to    talk to you

        C          D  Dsus  G
And make you un - der  -  stand,

G/B    C(add9)             Am7
    All you__ have to do is close your eyes

         C          D  Dsus  Em
And just reach out your   hands

     Am7            D7                    G    D/F♯  Em
And__ touch me, hold me close, don't ever let me go.
```

Chorus 2
```
         Am7     D7      G7       G7/B   C
More than words is all I ever needed you__ to show.

         Cm            G
Then you wouldn't have to say

         Em
That you love me,
```

Am7   D   D7♭9/A G
'Cause I'd al - read - y   know.

D/F♯
What would you do

Em   Bm   C
If my heart was torn in two?

G/B Am7
More than words to show you feel

D7   G
That your love for me is real.

D/F♯
What would you say

Em   Bm   C
If I took those words a-way?

G/B   Am7
Then you couldn't make things new

D7   G   G/B C(add9)
Just by say - ing "I love   you."

Am7
Outro   ‖: La, dee, da, dai, dai,

C
Dee, dai, dai, da.

D   Dsus G   G/B C(add9)
More than   words.   :‖ ***Play 3 times***

Am7
La, dee, da, dai, dai,

C
Dee, dai, dai, da.

D   Dsus G   D/F♯
More than   words.

Dm(add9)/F Esus
Oo, oo, oo, oo,

Am7   D
Oo, oo,   oo.

N.C.   G   Csus2 G/B Gm/B♭ Am7 G
More than words.

Mr. Jones

Words by Adam Duritz
Music by Adam Duritz and David Bryson

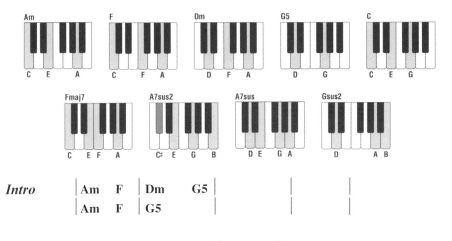

Intro |Am F |Dm G5 | | |
          |Am F |G5 | | |

Verse 1

    Am   **F** **Dm**
   I was down at the New Amsterdam

     G5
Staring at this yellow-haired girl.

   Am   **F**
Mr. Jones strikes up a conver-sation

   G5
With a black-haired flamenco dancer.

Am   **F**   **Dm**
She dances while his father plays gui-tar.

     G5
She's suddenly beautiful.

   Am   **F** **G5**
We all want something beautiful.

Man, I wish I was beautiful.

     Am   **F**
So come dance this silence down

        Dm **G5** **Am** **F** **G5**
Through the morning.

© 1993 EMI BLACKWOOD MUSIC INC. and JONES FALLS MUSIC
All Rights Controlled and Administered by EMI BLACKWOOD MUSIC INC.
All Rights Reserved   International Copyright Secured   Used by Permission

Verse 2

Am   F   Dm
   Cut up, Ma-ria!

                              G5   Am
Show me some of them Spanish dances.

                 F   G5
Pass me a bottle, Mr. Jones

Am   F   Dm
   Believe in me,

                 G5
Help me believe in anything.

         Am   F   G5
Cause' I want to be someone who believes.

Chorus 1

C   F   G5
   Mr. Jones and me

Tell each other fairy tales;

C   F
   Stare at the beautiful women.

        G5
"She's looking at you.

                        C
Ah, no, no, she's looking at me."

                F   G5
Smiling in the bright lights;

Coming through in stereo.

          C   F   G5
When__ ev'rybody loves__ you,

You can never be lonely.

Verse 3

Am   F Dm
I will paint my picture,

     G5
Paint myself in blue and red

       Am
And black and gray.

      F
All of the beautiful colors are

    G5
Very, ve-ry meaningful.

       Am   F
Yeah, well, you know gray is my favorite color

 Dm   G5
I__ felt so sym-bolic yesterday.

Am   F
 If I knew Pi-casso,

    G5   C
I would buy myself a gray guitar and play.

Chorus 2

C F   G5
Mr. Jones and me

Look into the future.

    C   F
Yeah, we stare at the beautiful women.

    G5
"She's looking at you.

Uh, I don't think so.

     C
She's lookin' at me."

     F
Standing in the spotlight,

G5
 I bought myself a gray guitar.

    C   F
When ev'rybody loves__ me,

G5   Am
 I will never be lone-ly.

Bridge

Am   Fmaj7
   I will never be lonely,

           Am   G5
Yes, I'm never gonna be lone - ly.

Am
   I want to be a lion.

Fmaj7   Am
   Ev'rybody wants to pass as cats.

We all want to be big, big stars,

     G5
Yeah, but   we got different reasons for that.

Am
   Believe in me.

      Fmaj7
'Cause I don't believe in anything,

    Am Asus2   Am   Asus   G5
And I   want to be some - one to__ believe.

C   F   G5
Chorus 3   Mr. Jones and me,

Stumbling through the barrio.

     C   F
Yeah, we__ stare at the beautiful women.

     G5
"She's per-fect for you.

                    C
Man, there's got to be somebody for me."

       F
I wanna be Bob Dy-lan.

    G5
Mr. Jones wishes he was someone

          C
Just a little more funk-y.

```
                    F                    G5
When ev'rybody loves you, ah, son,


That's just about as funky as you can be.



                C       F            G5
Chorus 4            Mr. Jones and me


Staring at the video.
                C               F
When I look at the tele-vision,

                G5
I want to see me


Starin' right back at me.

C                       F
    We all wanna be big stars,

                G5
But we don't know why


And we don't know how.

                C               F
But when ev'rybody loves__ me,

                G5
I'm gonna be just about as happy as I can be.

C       F               Gsus2
    Mr. Jones and me,


We're gonna be big stars.
```

Rainy Days and Mondays

Lyrics by Paul Williams
Music by Roger Nichols

Talk - in' to my - self ___ and feel - in' old,

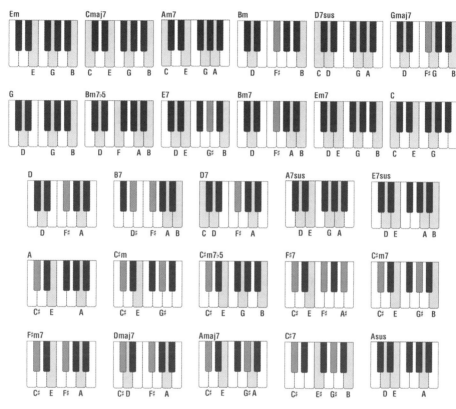

Intro
| Em   Cmaj7 G | Am7   Bm | Am7   D7sus |
| Gmaj7   D7sus | Gmaj7   D7sus |

Verse 1

G   Bm   Bm7♭5   E7
Talkin' to myself__ and feelin' old,

Am7   Bm7
Sometimes I'd like to quit.

Cmaj7   Bm7
Nothing ever seems to fit.

Copyright © 1970 ALMO MUSIC CORP.
Copyright Renewed
All Rights Reserved   Used by Permission

```
Em7          Cmaj7  Am7      C    G
Hangin' around,__      nothing to do but frown;

Am7                    C           G      D7sus  G  D7sus
Rainy days and Mondays al - ways get me__ down.
```

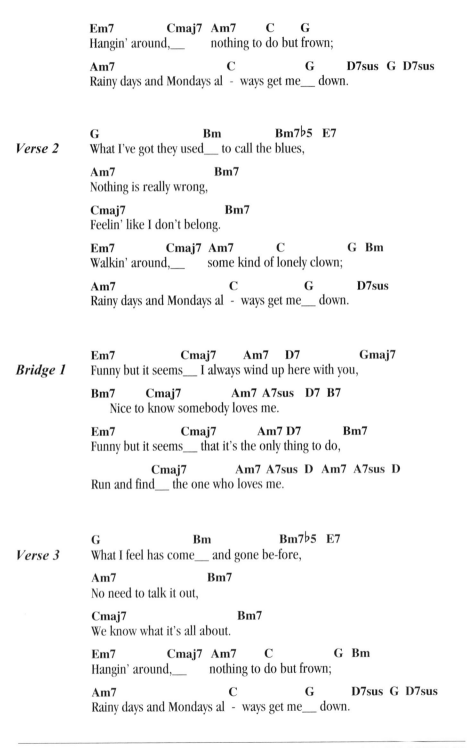

Verse 2
```
G                 Bm            Bm7♭5   E7
What I've got they used__ to call the blues,

Am7               Bm7
Nothing is really wrong,

Cmaj7              Bm7
Feelin' like I don't belong.

Em7          Cmaj7  Am7      C          G  Bm
Walkin' around,__      some kind of lonely clown;

Am7                    C         G       D7sus
Rainy days and Mondays al - ways get me__ down.
```

Bridge 1
```
Em7          Cmaj7     Am7  D7          Gmaj7
Funny but it seems__ I always wind up here with you,

Bm7     Cmaj7        Am7 A7sus  D7  B7
   Nice to know somebody loves me.

Em7          Cmaj7     Am7 D7        Bm7
Funny but it seems__ that it's the only thing to do,

        Cmaj7        Am7 A7sus  D  Am7  A7sus  D
Run and find__ the one who loves me.
```

Verse 3
```
G             Bm            Bm7♭5   E7
What I feel has come__ and gone be-fore,

Am7               Bm7
No need to talk it out,

Cmaj7                 Bm7
We know what it's all about.

Em7          Cmaj7  Am7      C          G  Bm
Hangin' around,__      nothing to do but frown;

Am7                    C           G      D7sus  G  D7sus
Rainy days and Mondays al - ways get me__ down.
```

Bridge 2

Em7   Cmaj7   Am7 D7   Gmaj7
Funny but it seems__ I always wind up here with you,

Bm7   Cmaj7   Am7 A7sus D7 B7
   Nice to know somebody loves me.

Em7   Cmaj7   Am7 D7   Bm7
Funny but it seems__ that it's the only thing to do,

         Cmaj7   Am7 A7sus D E7sus E7
Run and find__ the one who loves me.

Verse 5

A   C#m   C#m   F#7
What I feel has come and gone be - fore,

Bm7   C#m7
No need to talk it out,

Dmaj7   C#m7
We know what it's all about.

F#m7   Dmaj7 Bm7   E7sus   A C#m
Hangin' around,____ nothing to do but frown;

Bm7   E7sus   Amaj7 E7sus C#7
Rainy days and Mondays always get me down.

F#m7   Dmaj7 Bm7   E7sus   A C#m
Hangin' around,____ nothing to do but frown;

D   Bm7 C#m E7sus A   Bm7
Rainy days and Mondays al - ways get me__ down.

| Amaj7 Bm7 | Amaj7 Bm7 | Asus Amaj7 | |

One More Night

Words and Music by
Phil Collins

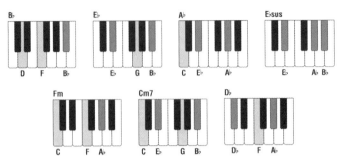

Intro

    B♭   **E♭**
One more night.

    B♭   **E♭**
One more night.

Verse 1

    A♭   **E♭sus**   **Fm**
I've been try - ing for so long

      B♭   **A♭**
To let you know,

        E♭sus   **Fm**
Let you know how I feel,

    A♭   **E♭sus**   **Fm**
And if I stum - ble, if I fall

      E♭
Just help me back,

    A♭   **E♭sus**   **Fm**
So I can make you   see.

Chorus 1

          B♭   **E♭**
Please give me one more night,

      B♭   **E♭**
Give me one more night.

    B♭   **E♭**
One more night,

© 1984 PHILIP COLLINS LTD. and HIT & RUN MUSIC (PUBLISHING) LTD.
All Rights Controlled and Administered by EMI APRIL MUSIC INC.
All Rights Reserved   International Copyright Secured   Used by Permission

Fm   Bb
'Cause I can't wait forever.

Bb   Eb
Give me just one more night,

Bb   Eb
Oh, just one more night,

Bb   Eb
Oh, one more night,

Fm   Bb
'Cause I can't wait forever.

Verse 2 Ab   Ebsus   Fm
I've been sit - ting here so long

Eb   Ab
Wasting time,

             Fm
Just staring at the phone,

Ab   Ebsus   Fm
And I was wond-'ring should I call__ you.

Eb
Then I thought,

Ab   Ebsus Fm
Maybe you're not a - lone.

Chorus 2 Bb   Eb
Please give me one more night,

Bb   Eb
Give me just one more night,

Bb   Eb
One more night.

Fm   Bb
'Cause I can't wait forever.

Bb   Eb
Please give me one more night,

       B♭   **E♭**
Oh, just one more night,

     B♭   **E♭**
Oh, one more night,

         Fm   **B♭**
'Cause I can't wait forever.

       B♭   **E♭**
Give me one more night,

        B♭   **E♭**
Give me just one more night,

     B♭   **E♭**
Just one more night

       Fm   **B♭**
'Cause I__ can't wait forev-er.

     Cm7   **E♭**   **Cm7**
Bridge   Like a riv - er to the sea,

        D♭   **Cm7**
I will al - ways be with you,

      E♭   **Cm7**
And if__ you sail away

       D♭
I will fol - low you.

       B♭   **E♭**
Chorus 3 Give me one more night,

        B♭   **E♭**
Give me just one more night,

     B♭   **E♭**
Oh, one more night

       Fm   **B♭**
'Cause I can't wait forever.

Verse 3

    A♭   E♭sus   Fm
I know there'll nev - er be a time

        E♭   A♭
You'll ever feel the same,

      E♭sus   Fm
And I know it's only right.

  A♭   E♭sus
But if you change__ your mind,

Fm   E♭
You know that   I'll be here,

A♭   E♭sus   Fm
And maybe we both can   learn.

Chorus 4

               B♭   E♭
Give me just one more night,

               B♭   E♭
Give me just one more night.

B♭   E♭
One more night,

          Fm   B♭
'Cause I can't wait forever.

               B♭   E♭
Give me just one more night,

               B♭   E♭
Give me just one more night,

  B♭   E♭
Oh, one more night,

          Fm   B♭
'Cause I can't wait forever.

Outro

B♭   E♭
‖: Oo, oo, oo.

B♭   E♭
Oo, oo, oo.

B♭   E♭
Oo, oo, oo.

Fm   B♭
Oo, oo, oo.   :‖   *Repeat and fade*

Push

Written by Rob Thomas
with Matt Serletic

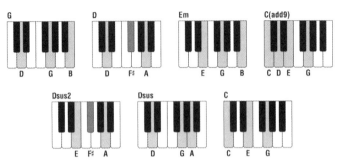

Intro ‖: G   D |Em   C(add9) :‖

Verse 1

         G   D   Em
She said, "I don't know if I've ever been good e-nough.

    C(add9)
I'm a little bit rusty,

G   D   Em C(add9)
And I think my head is caving in.

    G   D   Em
And I don't know if I've ever been really loved

    C(add9)
By a hand that's touched me.

G   D   Em
And I feel like something's go'n' to give,

      C(add9)
And I'm a little bit angry."

Dsus2
Oh, well. This ain't over, no, not here.

C(add9)   Dsus2
      Not while I still need you around.

You don't owe me.

© 1996 EMI BLACKWOOD MUSIC INC., BIDNIS, INC. (BMI) and MELUSIC (ASCAP)
All Rights for BIDNIS, INC. Controlled and Administered by EMI BLACKWOOD MUSIC INC.
All Rights Reserved   International Copyright Secured   Used by Permission

           C(add9)
We might change,__ yeah.

       D
Yeah, we just might feel good.

Chorus 1

  G   **Dsus**
I wanna push you around.

C(add9)   **D**
  Well, I will,   well, I will.

G   **Dsus**
I wanna push you down.

C(add9)   **D**
  Well, I will,   well, I will.

Em   **D**   **C** **D**
  I wanna take you for grant-ed.

Em   **D**   **C**
  I wanna take you for grant-ed,

     D   **G** **D** **Em** **C(add9)**
Yeah, yeah, I will, and I will,

     G   **D** **Em** **C(add9)**
And I__ will.

Verse 2

        G   **D**   **Em**
She said, "I don't know why you ever would lie to me."

         C(add9)
Like I'm a little untrusting

G   **D**   **Em** **C(add9)**
When I think that the truth is gonna hurt__ ya.

  G   **D**   **Em**
And I don't know why you couldn't just stay with__ me.

        C(add9)
You couldn't stand to be near me

G   **D**   **Em**
  When my face don't seem to want to shine

        C(add9)
'Cause it's a little bit dirty.

Dsus2
Oh, well. Well, don't just stand there,

C(add9)
Say nice things___ to me.

'Cause I've been cheated, I've been wronged.

Dsus2
And you, you don't know me.

C(add9)
Yeah, well, I can't change.

D
Well, I won't do anything at all.

Chorus 2   **Repeat Chorus 1**

       Em   **D**
Bridge   Oh, but don't bowl me over.

C   **D**   **Em**
Just wait a minute, well it kinda fell a-part.

      D **C** **N.C.**   **D**
Things get so crazy, cra - zy.

Em   **D**   **C(add9)** **D**
Don't rush this, ba-by.

Em   **D**   **C(add9)** **D**
Don't rush this, ba - by, ba - by.

Chorus 3
G   **Dsus**
I wanna push you around.

C(add9)   **D**
Well, I will,   well, I will.

G   **Dsus**
I wanna push you down.

C(add9)   **D**
Well, I will,   well, I will.

Em   **D**   **C** **D**
I wanna take you for grant-ed.

Em   **D**   **C(add9)**   **D**
I wanna take you, take you, yeah.

       G
Well, I will,   and I will,

D **Em**   **C**
I will,___ I will.

G   **D**   **Em**   **C**
And I will, I will,   I will.

      G D   **Em**
Yeah, I will___ push you around,

       C
He's wrapped___ you down.

G   **D**   **Em**
I wanna push you around,

C   **G**
Yeah, I will.

Runnin' Down a Dream

Words and Music by Tom Petty,
Jeff Lynne and Mike Campbell

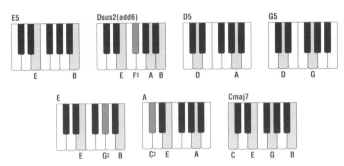

Intro   ‖: **E5** | :‖   *Play 4 times*

Verse 1

          E5
It was a beautiful day,

The sun beat down.

       Dsus2(add6)
I had the radio on,

      E5
I was driv - in'.

The trees flew by,

Me and Del were singin'

      Dsus2(add6)
Little "Runaway,"

      E5
I was fly - in'.

Copyright © 1989 Gone Gator Music, EMI April Music Inc. and Wild Gator Music
All Rights Reserved   Used by Permission

Chorus 1

      D5   **G5**   **E**
Yeah, runnin' down a dream

               G5   **A**
That never would come to me.

      D5   **G5**   **E**
Work - in' on a myste-ry;

           G5   **A**
Goin' wher-ever it leads.

          G5   **E5**
Runnin' down a dream.

Verse 2

      E5
I felt so good, like anything was possible,

        Dsus2(add6)
Hit cruise control

           E5
And rubbed my eyes.

The last three days

The rain was unstoppable.

        Dsus2(add6)
It was always cold,

        E5
No sun-shine.

Chorus 2   *Repeat Chorus 1*

	Cmaj7
Interlude	Woo.

        Dsus2(add6)
Woo.

        E5
Woo.

        Cmaj7
Woo.

        Dsus2(add6)
Woo.

        E5
Woo.

E5

Verse 3   I rolled on,

The sky grew dark.

        Dsus2(add6)
I put the pedal down

          E5
To make some time.

There's something good

Waitin' down this road.

        Dsus2(add6)
I'm pickin' up

        E5
Whatever is mine.

Chorus 3   ***Repeat Chorus 1***

Chorus 4   ***Repeat Chorus 1***

Outro   ***Repeat Interlude till fade***

Show Me the Way

Words and Music by
Peter Frampton

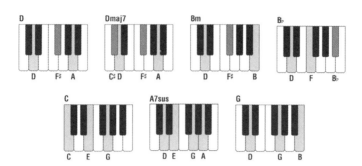

Intro ‖: D | Dmaj7 | Bm | B♭ C :‖ *Play 4 times*

Verse 1
    D
I wonder how you're feeling,

    Dmaj7
There's   ringing in my ears,

    Bm
And no one to relate to

    B♭   C
'Cept the sea.

D
Who can I believe in?

    Dmaj7
I'm   kneeling on the floor.

    Bm
There has to be a force,

    B♭
Who do___ I phone?

Copyright © 1975 ALMO MUSIC CORP. and NUAGES ARTISTS MUSIC LTD.
Copyright Renewed
All Rights Controlled and Administered by ALMO MUSIC CORP.
All Rights Reserved   Used by Permission

Bridge 1   **A7sus**
The stars around me shining,

      G
But all I really want to know...

      Bm
Chorus 1   Oh, won't you

      G
Show me the way,

Ev'ry day.

   Bm
I want you

      G   **G/A**
To show me the way, yeah.

Interlude 1 |D |Dmaj7 |Bm |B♭ C |

      D
Verse 2   Well, I can see no reason,

   Dmaj7
Your living on your nerves,

   Bm
When someone drops a cup,

   B♭   **C**
And I__ submerge.

   D
I'm swimming in a circle,

  Dmaj7
I   feel I'm going down.

   Bm
There has to be a fool

   B♭
To play__ my part.

| | **A7sus** |
| *Bridge 2* | Someone thought of healing |

G

But all I really want to know...

| | **Bm** |
| *Chorus 2* | Oh, won't you |

G

Show me the way,

Ev'ry day.

Bm

I want you

G

To show me the way, oh.

Bm

I want you

G   G/A

Day after day,   hey.

Solo	|D		|Dmaj7			
	|Bm		|B♭	|C	
	|D		|Dmaj7			
	|Bm		|G			

                          D
Verse 3   And I wonder if I'm dreaming,

                          Dmaj7
                I   feel so unashamed.

                          Bm   **B♭**
                I can't believe this is happening to me.

                          A7sus
Bridge 3   I watch you when you're sleeping,

                                G
                Oh, then I__ wanna take your love...

                                Bm
Chorus 3   Oh, won't you

                                G
                Show me the way,

                Ev'ry day.

                          Bm
                I want you

                                G
                To show me the way,

                One more time.

                          Bm
                I want you

                          G
                Day after day, hey.

                          Bm
                I want you

                          G   G/A
                Day after day,   hey.

Interlude 2 |D |Dmaj7 |Bm |G |

                      Bm
Chorus 4   I want you

                          G
              To show me the way

              Ev'ry day.

                  Bm
              I want you

                      G
              To show me the way

              Night and day.

                  Bm
              I want you

                      G   **G/A**
              Day after day,

                  D
              Hey, hey,

              Dmaj7   **Bm**   **B♭** **C**   **D**
              Oh.

Smooth

Words by Rob Thomas
Music by Rob Thomas and Itaal Shur

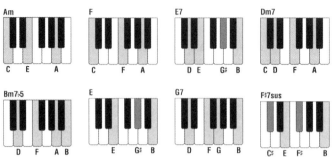

Intro ‖: Am   F   E7 | :‖ *Play 4 times*

Verse 1

           Am   **F E7**
Man, it's a hot one.

                Am   **F E7**
Like seven inches from the midday sun.

Well, I hear your whisper

       Dm7   **Bm7♭5** **E**
And the words melt ev'-ryone.

         Am   **F E7**
But you stay so__ cool.

      Am   **F E7**
My Mune-quita,

            Am   **F E7**
My Spanish Harlem Mona Lisa.

            Dm7   **Bm7♭5**
Well, you're my reason for__ reason,

E   **Am**   **F E7**
The step in my groove.

© 1999 EMI BLACKWOOD MUSIC INC., BIDNIS, INC. and ITAAL SHUR MUSIC
All Rights for BIDNIS, INC. Controlled and Administered by EMI BLACKWOOD MUSIC INC.
All Rights Reserved   International Copyright Secured   Used by Permission

Chorus 1   **Am**   **F** **E7**
And if you said__ this life__ ain't__ good enough,

      Am   **F E7**
I would give my world to lift you up.

       Am **F E7**   **Dm7** **Bm7♭5**
I could change my life to better suit your mood

G7   **F#7sus** **E7**
Because you're so__ smooth.

      Am   **F** **E7**
Well, and it's just like the o-cean under the moon.

      Am   **F**   **E7**
Well, it's the same as the emo-tion that I get from you.

   Am   **F**   **E7**
You got the kind of lov-in' that can be so smooth, yeah.

Dm7 N.C.   **E7**
Gimme your heart, make it real.

N.C.
Or else forget about it.

Interlude ‖: **Am** **F** **E7** | :‖

Verse 2

           Am   **F** **E7**
Well, I'll tell you one thing,

                     Am   **F** **E7**
If you would leave it'd be a cryin' shame.

           Dm7
In ev'ry breath and ev'ry word

   Dm7   **Bm7♭5**   **E**   **Am**   **F** **E7**
I hear_____ your name callin' me   out,   yeah.

             Am   **F** **E7**
Well, out from the barrio

                  Am   **F** **E7**
You hear my rhythm on your radio.

             Dm7
And you feel the turning of the world,

   Dm7   **Bm7♭5**   **E**
So__ soft and slow,

         Am   **F E7**
Turnin' you__ round   and round.

Chorus 2   ***Repeat Chorus 1***

Solo   ‖:**Am**   **F**   **E7** | :‖   ***Play 7 times***
          |**Dm7**   **Bm7♭5** | **G7** |**F♯7sus**   **E7** | |

Chorus 3   ***Repeat Chorus 1***

Outro   ***Repeat Chorus 1 (Instrumental) till fade***

Sorry Seems to Be the Hardest Word

Words and Music by Elton John
and Bernie Taupin

Melody:

What have I got to do to make you love ___ me ___

Gm   Cm7   F   Bb   Am7b5   D7

D   Em7b5   Cm   C7   Eb

F7   D7b9   Ebm7b5   D7sus   Gm(add9)

Verse 1

Gm　　　　　　　　　　　　Cm7
What have I got to do to make you love___ me?

F　　　　　　　　　　　　　　Bb　Am7b5　D7
What have I got to do to make you care?

Gm　　　　　　　　　　Cm7
What do I do when lightning strikes___ me

F　　　　　　　　　　　　　Bb　Am7b5　D7
And I wake to find that you're not there?

Gm　　　　　　　　　　　Cm7
What do I do to make you want___ me?

F　　　　　　　　　　　　Bb　Am7b5　D7
What have I gotta do to be heard?

Gm　　　　　　　　　　Cm7
What do I say when it's all o - ver?

F　　　　　　　　　　Bb　F
Sorry seems to be the hardest word.

Copyright © 1976 HST MGT. LTD. and ROUGE BOOZE, INC.
Copyright Renewed
All Rights for HST MGT. LTD. in the United States and Canada Controlled and Administered by
UNIVERSAL - SONGS OF POLYGRAM INTERNATIONAL, INC.
All Rights for ROUGE BOOZE, INC. in the United States and Canada Controlled and Administered by
UNIVERSAL - POLYGRAM INTERNATIONAL PUBLISHING, INC.
All Rights Reserved   Used by Permission

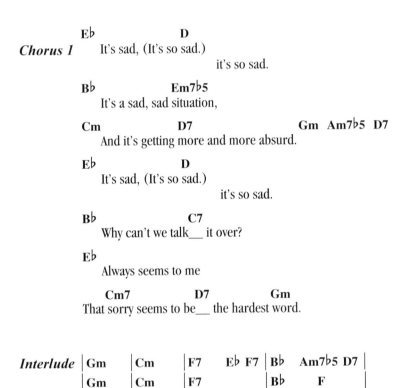

Chorus 1

> Eb   D
> It's sad, (It's so sad.)
>
>   it's so sad.
>
> Bb   Em7b5
> It's a sad, sad situation,
>
> Cm   D7   Gm Am7b5 D7
> And it's getting more and more absurd.
>
> Eb   D
> It's sad, (It's so sad.)
>
>   it's so sad.
>
> Bb   C7
> Why can't we talk__ it over?
>
> Eb
> Always seems to me
>
> Cm7   D7   Gm
> That sorry seems to be__ the hardest word.

Interlude | Gm | Cm | F7 Eb F7 | Bb Am7b5 D7 |
      | Gm | Cm | F7 | Bb F |

<pre>
                 E♭   D
Chorus 2   It's sad, (It's so sad.)
                                    it's so sad.

             B♭   Em7♭5
             It's a sad, sad situation,

             Cm   D7   Gm Am7♭5 D7
             And it's getting more and more absurd.

             E♭   D
             It's sad, (It's so sad.)
                                    it's so sad.

             B♭   C7
             Why can't we talk__ it over?

             E♭
             Always seems to me

             Cm7   D7   Gm
       That sorry seems to be__ the hardest word.

                             Cm7
       What do I do to make you love__ me?

       F   B♭
             What have I gotta do to be heard?

       Gm   Cm
             What do I do when lightning strikes me?

       Am7♭5   D7♭9
       What have I got to do,

       Gm   Cm
       What have I got to do?

       Am7♭5   D7   B♭   E♭m7♭5 Cm Gm
       Sorry seems to be__ the hardest word.

      │Am7♭5   D7sus D7 │Gm(add9)   │
</pre>

So Far Away

Words and Music by
Carole King

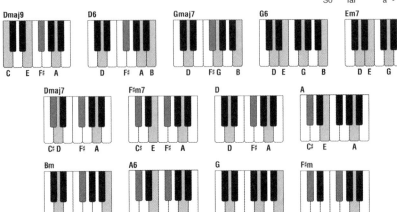

Intro ‖: **Dmaj9 D6** | **Dmaj9 D6** :‖

Dmaj9 D6

Chorus 1 So far a - way.

Dmaj9   **D6**   **Gmaj7**   **G6**
Doesn't anybody stay in one place__ anymore?

Em7   **G**   **Dmaj7 G Dmaj7**
It would be so fine to see your face at   my door.

Gmaj7   **F♯m7**   **Em7 G**   **Dmaj9 D6**
It doesn't help__ to know__   you're just   time a-way.

Dmaj9   **D6**   **Gmaj7**   **G6**
Long ago, I reached for you and   there you stood.

Em7   **G**   **Dmaj7 G Dmaj7**
Holding you again__ could only do   me__ good.

Gmaj7 **F♯m7** **Em7**   **G**   **Dmaj9**   **D6**
How I wish__ I   could, but you're so   far a-way.

|**Dmaj9**   **D A** |

Bm   **A6**   **G**   **D**

Verse 1 One more song about a movin' along the highway.

Em7   **G**   **Dmaj7**
Can't say much of anything that's new.

© 1971 (Renewed 1999) COLGEMS-EMI MUSIC INC.
All Rights Reserved   International Copyright Secured   Used by Permission

PIANO CHORD SONGBOOK

```
       F#m        F#m7          Em7
If I could only work this life out__ my way,

      G          Bm      Em7        G
I'd rather spend it    bein' close to you.
```

```
                    Dmaj9    D6
Chorus 2   But you're so      far a-way.
```

```
           Dmaj9          D6          Gmaj7      G6
Doesn't anybody stay in one place__ anymore?
```

```
           Em7        G              Dmaj7 G   Dmaj7
It would be so fine to see your face at  my   door.
```

```
            Gmaj7    F#m7     Em7 G      Dmaj9     D6
It doesn't help__ to know__   you're so      far a-way.
```

```
           Dmaj9  D6        Gmaj7    G6  Em7  G
             Yeah,__ you're so__   far a-way.
```

```
           G                  A6              G
Verse 2    Travelin' around sure gets me down and lonely.
```

```
           Em7        G            Dmaj7
Nothin' else to do__ but close my mind.
```

```
            F#m7                      Em7
I sure hope the road don't come to__ own me.
```

```
             G            Bm     Em7      G
There's so many dreams__ I've yet to find.
```

```
                    Dmaj9    D6
Chorus 3   But you're so      far a-way.
```

```
           Dmaj9          D6          Gmaj7      G6
Doesn't anybody stay in one place__ anymore?
```

```
               Em7        G           Dmaj7   G   Dmaj7
It would be   so fine__ to see your face  at  my   door,
```

```
             Gmaj7    F#m7     Em7 G      Dmaj9     D6
And it doesn't help__ to know__   you're so      far a-way.
```

```
           Dmaj9  D6        Gmaj7    G6
             Yeah,__ you're so__   far a-way.
```

```
           Em7    G          Dmaj9    D6  Dmaj9  D6
             Hey,__ you're so      far____  away.
```

```
Outro      ‖: Gmaj7  G6  | Em7  G   |          |
             | Dmaj9  D6  |Dmaj9  D6   :‖    Repeat and fade
```

Still the Same

Words and Music by
Bob Seger

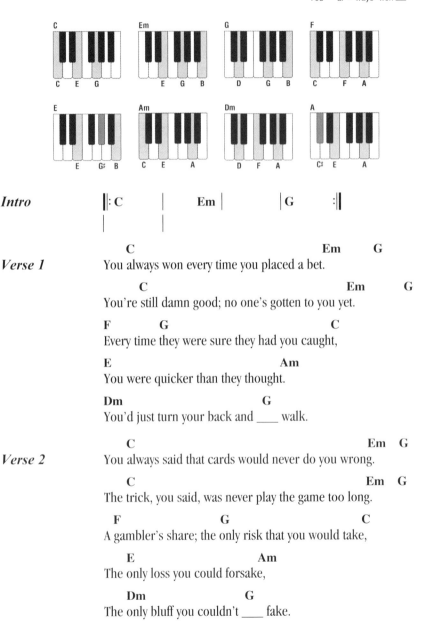

Intro ‖: C | Em | G :‖
| |

Verse 1

        C   Em   G
You always won every time you placed a bet.

             C   Em   G
You're still damn good; no one's gotten to you yet.

F   G   C
Every time they were sure they had you caught,

E   Am
You were quicker than they thought.

Dm   **G**
You'd just turn your back and ___ walk.

Verse 2

       C   Em   G
You always said that cards would never do you wrong.

       C   Em   G
The trick, you said, was never play the game too long.

 F   G   C
A gambler's share; the only risk that you would take,

 E   Am
The only loss you could forsake,

   Dm   **G**
The only bluff you couldn't ___ fake.

Copyright © 1977, 1978 Gear Publishing Co.
Copyright Renewed
All Rights Reserved   Used by Permission

Chorus 1

                    C
And you're still the same.

   E   A
I caught up with you yesterday.

               Dm
Moving game to game;

                    G
No one standing in your way.

                C
Turning on the charm

E   A
Long enough to get you by.

               Dm   G
You're still the same, ___ you still aim ___ high.

Piano Solo

‖: C | | Em | G   :‖

Verse 3

F   G   C
There you stood; ev'rybody watched you play.

E   Am
I just turned and walked away.

Dm   G
I had nothing left to say.

	C
Chorus 2	'Cause you're still the same.

                                                     Em   G

(Still the same, baby, babe, you're still the same.)

                  C

You're still the same.

                                                     Em   G

(Still the same, baby, babe, you're still the same.)

                    C

 Moving game to game.

                                                   Em   G

(Still the same, baby, babe, you're still the same.)

                      C

Some things never change.

                                                   Em   G

(Still the same, baby, babe, you're still the same.)

                    C

Ah, you're still the same.

                                                   Em   G

(Still the same, baby, babe, you're still the same.)

                  C

Still the same.

                                                 Em   G

(Still the same, baby, babe, you're still the same.)   *Fade out*

Summer of '69

Words and Music by Bryan Adams
and Jim Vallance

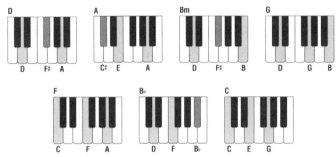

Intro | D | | |

Verse 1

D
I got my first real six-string;

A
Bought it at the five and dime.

D
Played it 'til my fingers bled;

A
Was the summer of sixty-nine.

Verse 2

D
Me and some guys from school

A
Had a band and we tried real hard.

D
Jimmy quit, and Jody got married;

A
I should-a known we'd never get far.

Copyright © 1984 IRVING MUSIC, INC., ADAMS COMMUNICATIONS, INC., ALMO MUSIC CORP. and TESTATYME MUSIC
All Rights for ADAMS COMMUNICATIONS, INC. Controlled and Administered by IRVING MUSIC, INC.
All Rights for TESTATYME MUSIC Controlled and Administered by ALMO MUSIC CORP.
All Rights Reserved   Used by Permission

Chorus 1

Bm   A
Oh, when I look back now,

D   G
That summer seemed to last forever,

Bm   A
And if I had the choice,

D   G
Yeah, I'd always wanna be there.

Bm   A   D   A
Those were the best days of my life.

Verse 3

D
Ain't no use in complainin'

A
When you got a job to do.

D
Spend my evenin's down at the drive-in,

A
And that's when I met you.

Chorus 2

Bm   A
Standin' on your mama's porch,

D   G
You told me that you'd wait forever.

Bm   A
Oh, and when you held my hand,

D   G
I knew that it was now or never.

Bm   A   D   A
Those were the best days of my life.

                     D   A
Back in the summer of sixty-nine.

Bridge

    F   B♭
Man, we were killin' time,

        C
We were young and restless,

    B♭   F
We needed to unwind.

      B♭   C
I guess nothin' can last forev - er,

Forever, no!

Interlude   ***Repeat Verse 1 (Instrumental)***

Verse 4

D
And now the times are changin';

A
Look at ev'rything that's come and gone.

D
Sometimes when I play that old six-string

A
I think about you, wonder what went wrong.

Chorus 3

Bm   A
Standin' on your mama's porch,

D   G
You told me that it'd last forever.

Bm   A
Oh, and when you held my hand,

D   G
I knew that it was now or never.

Bm   A   D   A
Those were the best days of my life.

                 D   A
Back in the summer of sixty-nine.

                 D   A
‖: It was the summer of sixty-nine.   :‖   ***Repeat and fade***

Surrender

Words and Music by
Rick Nielsen

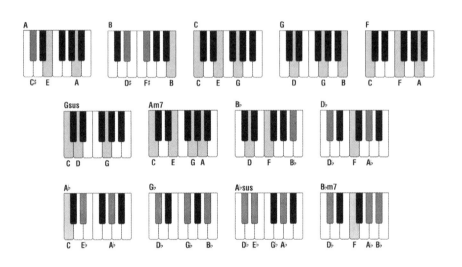

Intro ‖: A | | B | :‖

Verse 1

       C   G

Mother told me, yes,___ she told me

       F   C

I'd meet girls like you.

                              G

She also told me, "Stay away,

             F   C

You'll never know what you'll catch."

© 1978 SCREEN GEMS-EMI MUSIC INC. and ADULT MUSIC
All Rights Controlled and Administered by SCREEN GEMS-EMI MUSIC INC.
All Rights Reserved   International Copyright Secured   Used by Permission

<pre>
                    F   Gsus   C
Pre-Chorus 1   Just the other day__ I heard a sol - diers falling off

                          F   Gsus   C
               Some In - donesian junk__ that's going 'round.

                    C
Chorus 1   Mommy's alright,

                    Am7
               Daddy's alright,

                    Gsus   F
               They just seem a little weird.

                        C   Am7
               Surren - der, surren - der,

                        Gsus   F
               But don't__ give yourself away,

               Ay, ay, ay.

Interlude   ‖: Bb | | C | :‖

                    C   G
Verse 2   Father says, "Your mother's right,

                        F   C
               She's really up on things.

               Before we married,

                    G   F   C
               Mom - my served in the WACS__ in the Philippines.
</pre>

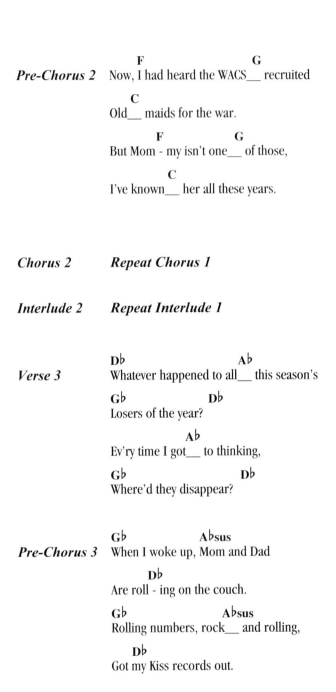

Pre-Chorus 2
          F   G
Now, I had heard the WACS__ recruited

       C
Old__ maids for the war.

            F   G
But Mom - my isn't one__ of those,

          C
I've known__ her all these years.

Chorus 2   **Repeat Chorus 1**

Interlude 2   **Repeat Interlude 1**

Verse 3
       D♭   A♭
Whatever happened to all__ this season's

       G♭   D♭
Losers of the year?

           A♭
Ev'ry time I got__ to thinking,

       G♭   D♭
Where'd they disappear?

Pre-Chorus 3
       G♭   A♭sus
When I woke up, Mom and Dad

           D♭
Are roll - ing on the couch.

       G♭   A♭sus
Rolling numbers, rock__ and rolling,

          D♭
Got my Kiss records out.

Chorus 3

Db
Mommy's alright,

Bbm7
Daddy's alright,

    Absus   Gb
They just seem a little weird.

    Db   Bbm7
Surren - der, surren - der,

     Absus   Gb
But don't___ give yourself away,

Ay, ay, ay.

    Db Gb Db Ab
Away.

    Db Gb Db Ab
Away.

    Db
‖: Surren - der,

    (Mommy's alright.)

    Bbm7
Surren - der,

    (Daddy's alright.)

    Absus   Gb
But don't___ give yourself away. :‖   ***Repeat and fade***

Tempted

Words and Music by Christopher Difford
and Glenn Tilbrook

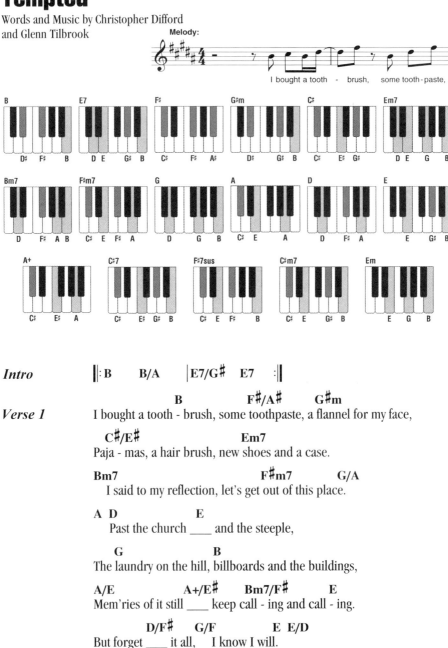

Intro ‖: B   B/A | E7/G♯   E7   :‖

                 B   **F♯/A♯**   **G♯m**

Verse 1   I bought a tooth - brush, some toothpaste, a flannel for my face,

        C♯/E♯   **Em7**
        Paja - mas, a hair brush, new shoes and a case.

     Bm7   **F♯m7**   **G/A**
        I said to my reflection, let's get out of this place.

     A D   **E**
        Past the church ____ and the steeple,

        G   **B**
        The laundry on the hill, billboards and the buildings,

     A/E   **A+/E♯**   **Bm7/F♯**   **E**
        Mem'ries of it still ____ keep call - ing and call - ing.

                D/F♯   **G/F**   **E E/D**
        But forget ____ it all,   I know I will.

© 1981 EMI MUSIC PUBLISHING LTD.
All Rights in the United States and Canada Controlled and Administered by EMI BLACKWOOD MUSIC INC.
All Rights Reserved   International Copyright Secured   Used by Permission

Chorus 1

B   B/A   E7/G# E7
Tempted by the fruit of anoth - er,

B   B/A   E7/G#
Tempted, but the truth is discov - ered.

E7   C#7   F#7sus4
What's been goin' on, and now that you have gone,

B B/A
There's no oth - er.

E7/G#   E7   B B/A
Tempted by the fruit of anoth - er,

E7/G#   E7   C#m7   Em
Tempted, but the truth is discov - ered.

Verse 2

B   F#/A#   G#m
I'm at the car - park, the airport, the baggage carousel,

C#/E#   Em7
The people keep on grabbin', ain't wishin' I was well.

Bm7   F#m7   G/A
I said, "It's no occasion, it's no story I can tell."

A D   E   G
At my bed - side, empty pockets, a foot without a sock.

B   A/E   A+/E#
Your body gets much closer, I fumble for the clock,

Bm7/F#   E   D/F# G/F   E E/D
Alarm - ed by the seduc - tion, I wish   that it would stop.

Chorus 2   *Repeat Chorus 1*

Verse 3

B   F#/A#   G#m7
I bought a nov - el, some perfume, a fortune all for you,

C#/E#   Em7
But it's not my conscience that hates to be untrue.

Bm7   F#m7   G/A A D
I asked of my reflection, tell me what is there to do?

Chorus 3

B   B/A   E7/G# E7
Tempted by the fruit of anoth - er,

B   B/A   E7/G#
Tempted, but the truth is discov - ered.

E7   C#7   F#7sus4
  What's been goin' on, now that you have gone,

              B B/A
There's no oth - er.

E7/G#   E7   B B/A
Tempted by the fruit of anoth - er,

E7/G#   E7   C#m7
Tempted, but the truth is dis - covered.

Outro

   B   B/A   E7/G# E7
‖: Tempted by the fruit of anoth - er,

B   B/A   E7/G# E7
Tempted but the truth is discov - ered. :‖ *Repeat and fade*

Time After Time

Words and Music by Cyndi Lauper
and Rob Hyman

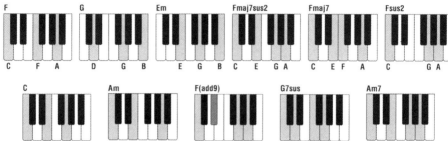

Intro
```
| F      | G      | Em     | F    Fmaj7sus2  Fmaj7  |
| F      | G      | Em     | Fsus2           Fmaj7sus2  |
```

Verse 1

F   C   F   C   F   C   F   C
Lyin' in my bed I hear the clock tick and think of you.

F   C F   C   F C   F   C
Caught up in cir - cles confu - sion is nothing new.

F   G Em   F
Flashback,   warm nights,

        G   Em
Almost left behind.

F   G   Em   F
Suitcase___ of memories,

        G
Time after.

Verse 2

F   C   F   C
Some-times you picture me,

       F   C   F   C
I'm walk - ing too far a - head.

F   C   F C
You're calling to   me,

F   C   F   C
Can't hear what you've said.

Copyright © 1983 Rellla Music Co., WB Music Corp. and Dub Notes
All Rights for Rellla Music Co. Administered by Sony/ATV Music Publishing LLC, 8 Music Square West, Nashville, TN 37203
All Rights for Dub Notes Administered by WB Music Corp.
International Copyright Secured   All Rights Reserved

```
              F       G  Em      F
         Then you say___ go slow,

               G           Em
         I fall__ behind.

         F         G           Em          F
            The sec - ond hand__ unwinds.


                          G
Chorus 1     If you're lost,___ you can look

                    Am
         And you will__ find me,

         F(add9) G7sus      C
            Time after time.

                    G
         If you fall__ I will catch you,

                 Am
         I'll be__ waiting,

         F(add9) G7sus      C
            Time after time.

                       G
         If you're lost,___ you can look

                    Am
         And you will__ find me,

         F(add9) G7sus      C
            Time after time.

                    G
         If you fall__ I will catch you,

                 Am
         I'll be__ waiting,

         F(add9) G7sus      C
            Time after time.


Solo         Repeat Intro


         F   C    F     C
Verse 3      Af - ter my picture fades

                 F    C     F      C
         And dark - ness has turned to gray.
```

```
        F        C         F     C
Watch - ing through win - dows,

              F      C        F     C
You're wonder-ing if I'm__ O.__K.

F       G    Em    F
Secrets__    sto - len

                G          Em
From deep__ inside.

F                G           Em          F
    The drum__ beats out__ of time.
```

```
                       G
```
Chorus 2   If you're lost,__ you can look

```
                  Am
```
And you will__ find me,

```
F(add9)  G7sus       C
```
    Time after time.

```
              G
```
If you fall__ I will catch you,

```
          Am
```
I'll be__ waiting,

```
F(add9)  G7sus       C
```
    Time after time.

Interlude   ‖: G |Am7 |F(add9) G7sus |C   :‖   *Play 3 times*

```
              F     G    Em      F
```
Verse 4   Then you say__ go slow,

```
              G          Em
```
I fall__ behind.

```
F        G          Em          F
```
    The sec - ond hand__ unwinds.

Chorus 3   **Repeat Chorus 1**

```
          F(add9)      G7sus    C
```
Outro   ‖:   Time after time.   :‖   *Repeat and fade*

Time for Me to Fly

Words and Music by
Kevin Cronin

I've been a - round _ for _ you, I've

Intro   ‖: D   G(add9) │ A(add4)   G(add9)   :‖

Verse 1
        D
I've been around for you,

            A(add4)
I've been up and down for you,

            G(add9)   **D   G(add9)/D   D   G(add9)/D   D**
But I__ just can't get any relief.

I've swallowed my pride for you,

A(add4)
    Lived and lied for you,

        G(add9)   **D   G(add9)/D   D   G(add9)/D   D**
But a you still make me feel like a thief.

              A(add4)
You got me stealin' your love away

            G(add9)   D
'Cause a you never give it.

    A(add4)
Peelin' the years away

            G(add9)   D
And a we can't re-live it.

      G(add9)   D
Oh, I make you laugh,

           G(add9)   D
And a you make me cry.

    A(add4)
    I believe it's time for me to fly.

Copyright © 1978 Fate Music (ASCAP)
International Copyright Secured   All Rights Reserved

‖: D   G(add9) |A(add4)   G(add9) :‖

             D
Verse 2   You said we'd work it out,

              A(add4)
You said that you had no doubt,

              G(add9)   D   G(add9)/D   D   G(add9)/D
That deep down we were really in love.

              D
Oh, but I'm tired of holdin' on

              A(add4)
To feelin' I know is gone.

          G(add9)   D   G(add9)/D   D   G(add9)/D
    I do believe that I've had enough.

              D   A(add4)
I've had e-nough of the falseness

              G(add9)   D
Of a worn - out re-lation.

              A(add4)
E-nough of the jealousy

              G(add9)   D
And the intolera - tion.

              G(add9)   D
Oh, I make you laugh,

              G(add9)   D
And a you make me cry.

          A(add4)   D   G(add9)   D   NC.
    I believe it's time for me to fly.

                         A(add4)   G(add9)   D
Chorus 1   (Time for me to fly.)

                            Oh, I've got to set__ myself free.

                         A(add4)   G(add9) D
    (Time for me to fly.)

                            Ah, that's just how it's a got to be.

G(add9)   A(add4)
  I know it hurts to say good-bye,

         G(add9) A(add4)
But it's time for me to fly.

Interlude | D | | G(add9) | | |
     | A(add4) | | D | |

         A(add4)   G(add9) D
Chorus 2 (Time for me to fly.)

           Oh, I've got to set__ myself free.
        A(add4)   G(add9) D
(Time for me to fly.)

          Ah, that's just how it's a got to be.
G(add9)   A(add4)
  I know it hurts to say good-bye,

        G(add9) A(add4)
But it's time for me to fly.

      G(add9) A5
It's time for me to fly,__ ee-i, ee-i.

       D
It's time for me to fly.

    G(add9) A(add4)
(It's time for me to fly.)

    G(add9) D
It's time for me to fly.

       A(add4)
(It's time for me to fly.)

    G(add9) D
It's time for me to fly.

    G(add9)   A(add4) G(add9) D
(It's time for me to fly.)

       Babe,__ it's time for me to fly.

What a Fool Believes

Words and Music by Michael McDonald
and Kenny Loggins

Melody:

He came from some-where back in her long __

A7 · G(add9) · D · Em7 · F#m7 · Bbdim

Bm7 · Bb9 · Gmaj7 · Dmaj7 · C7 · B7

G#m7b5 · Gm7 · Bb · F · Dm7 · Bb5

Intro

‖: A7   Gadd9   D/F# | |

| Em7 F#m7 Gadd9 Bbdim Bm7 | Bb9 :‖

Verse 1

A7   Gadd9   D/F#
He came from somewhere back in her long ago,

Em7 F#m7 Gadd9 Bbdim Bm7   Bb9
          The senti - men - tal fool don't see,

A7   Gadd9   D/F#
Tryin' hard ___ to recre - ate what had yet to be created

Em7 F#m7 Gadd9 Bbdim Bm7
          Once in her   life.

Verse 2

Bb9   A7   Gadd9   D/F#
She musters a smile   for his nostalgic tale,

Em7 F#m7 Gadd9 Bbdim Bm7   Bb9   A7
          Never   com - in' near what he wanted to say,

Gadd9 D/F#   Em7 F#m7 Gadd9 Bbdim Bm7
Only to realize   it never   real - ly was.

Copyright © 1978 Snug Music and Milk Money Music
All Rights for Snug Music Administered by Wixen Music Publishing, Inc.
All Rights Reserved   Used by Permission

Pre-Chorus 1

Bm7   A7
She had a place in his life.

Bm7   A7
He never made her think ___ twice.

       Em7   Gmaj7/A Dmaj7
As he rises   to her   apology,

C7   B7   Em7   Gmaj7/A Bm7
An - ybod - y else would surely know

          G#m7♭5
He's watching her go.

Chorus 1

                   Gm7   B♭/C
But what a fool believes ___ he sees,

                   F   Dm7
No wise man has the pow - er to reason away.

B♭5/D♭ B♭5/C B♭5/B B♭5 F/A   Gm7
                              What seems

     B♭/C   F
To be ___ is always better than noth - ing.

             Dm7 B♭5/D♭ B♭5/C B♭5/B B♭5
And nothing at all ___   keeps ___ sending him

Verse 3

A7   Gadd9   D/F#
Somewhere back in her long ago,

Em7 F#m7   Gadd9 B♭dim Bm7
     Where he can   still   believe

       B♭9   A7
There's a place in her life.

Gadd9 D/F#   Em7 F#m7 Gadd9 B♭dim Bm7
Someday, ___ somehow,   she will re - turn.

Pre-Chorus 2   *Repeat Pre-Chorus 1*

                                    Gm7   **B♭/C**
Chorus 2   But what a fool believes ___ he sees,

                                        F   **Dm7**
                No wise man has the pow - er to reason a - way.

                B♭5/D♭ B♭5/C B♭5/B B♭5 F/A   Gm7
                                      What seems

                        B♭/C   **F**
                To be ___ is always better than noth - ing

                        Dm7
                And nothing at all.

                 B♭5/D♭ B♭5/C B♭5/B B♭5   F/A   Gm7   B♭/C
Outro/Chorus ‖:   What   a fool ___ believes ___ he sees,

                                        F   **Dm7**
                No wise man has the pow - er to reason away.

                B♭5/D♭ B♭5/C B♭5/B B♭5 F/A   Gm7   B♭/C
                                      What seems ___ to be

                                        F
                Is always better than noth - ing

                        Dm7
                And nothing at all.   :‖   *Repeat and fade w/Vocal ad lib.*

Walking in Memphis

Words and Music by
Marc Cohn

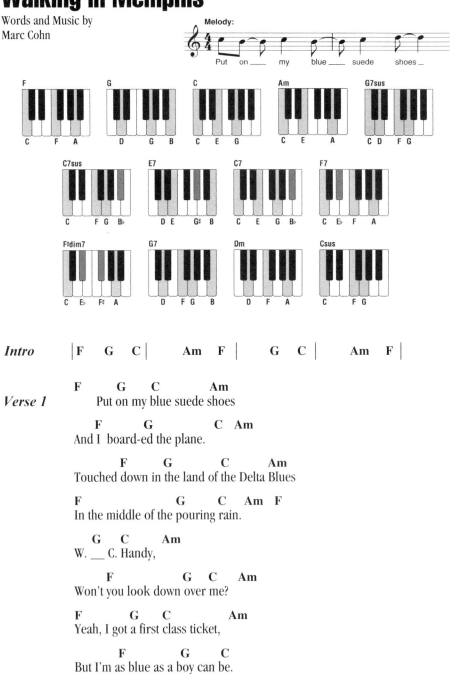

Melody:

Put on __ my blue __ suede shoes __

Intro | F G C | Am F | G C | Am F |

Verse 1

      F   G   C   Am
Put on my blue suede shoes

        F   G   C Am
And I board-ed the plane.

           F   G   C   Am
Touched down in the land of the Delta Blues

F   G   C   Am F
In the middle of the pouring rain.

      G   C   Am
W. __ C. Handy,

         F   G C   Am
Won't you look down over me?

F   G   C   Am
Yeah, I got a first class ticket,

        F   G   C
But I'm as blue as a boy can be.

Copyright © 1991 Sony/ATV Music Publishing LLC
All Rights Administered by Sony/ATV Music Publishing LLC, 8 Music Square West, Nashville, TN 37203
International Copyright Secured   All Rights Reserved

Chorus 1

      Am   **F**   **G** **C**
Then I'm walking in Mem - phis,

Am   **F**   **G**   **C**
I was walking with my feet ten feet off of Beale.

Am   **F**   **G** **C**
    Walking in Mem - phis,

Am   **F**   **G**   **G7sus** **C**
But do I really feel the way I feel?

Verse 2

G7sus   **C**
   Saw the ghost of El - vis

G7sus   **C**
   On Union Ave-nue.

      G7sus   **C**
Followed him up   to the gates of Grace - land,

    G7sus   **C**
Then I watched him walk right through.

      F   **G**   **C**
Now, se-curity, they did not see him.

Am **F**   **G**   **C**
They just   hovered 'round his tomb

Am   **F**   **G**
But there's a pretty little thing

    C   **Am**
Wait-ing for the King,

F   **N.C.**
Down in the Jungle Room.

C
When I was walking in Memphis.

Chorus 2

Am   **F**   **G** **C**
Then I'm walking in Mem - phis,

Am   **F**   **G**   **C**
I was walking with my feet ten feet off of Beale.

Am   **F**   **G** **C**
    Walking in Mem - phis,

Am   **F**   **G**   **C7sus** **C7** **C7sus** **C7**
But do I really feel the way I feel?

Bridge

          C7sus   C7   C7sus C7
They've got   catfish on the table.

          C7sus   C7   C7sus C7
They've got gospel in the air.

               E7   F7
And Reverend Green__ be glad to see you

        F#dim7   G7   N.C.
When you haven't got a prayer.

                            F   G   C
But, boy, you got a prayer in Mem - phis.

| | Am F | G   C | Am F |

Verse 3

F   G   C Am
Now, Muriel plays pia-no

     F   G   C   Am
Ev'ry Friday at the Holly-wood.

F   G   C   Am
And they brought me down to see her,

F   G C   Am
And they asked me if I   would

F   G   C   Am
    Do a little num - ber.

      F   G   C   Am
And I   sang with all my might.

        F   G   C   Am
She said,   "Tell me, are you a Christian, child?"

         F N.C.   C
And I said,   "Ma'am, I am to-night."

```
                        F    G   C
Chorus 3     Walking in Mem - phis,

             Am              F      G       C
             I was walking with my feet ten feet off of Beale.

             Am             F     G   C
                 Walking in Mem - phis,

             Am          F     C  Dm C
             But do I really feel the way I    feel?

                 Am              F
             Walk - ing in Mem - phis,

             Am              F      G       C
             I was walking with my feet ten feet off of Beale.

             Am             F     G   C
                 Walking in Mem - phis,

             Am          F     G    Csus
             But do I really feel the way I feel?

             |    G    C |    Am   F  |    G    C  |    Am    F  |


             F    G    C       Am
Outro            Put on my blue suede shoes

                 F       G          C   Am
             And I board-ed the plane.

                     F      G        C       Am
             Touched down in the land of the Delta Blues

             F              G      C     Am
             In the middle of the pouring rain.

                     F      G        C       Am
             Touched down in the land of the Delta Blues

                 F                G    F
             In the middle of the pour - ing rain.

             |F    G    C |    Am   F  |    G    C  |    Am    F  |

             |    G    C |    Am   |F    G   |C           |
```

What I Like About You

Words and Music by Michael Skill,
Wally Palamarchuk and James Marinos

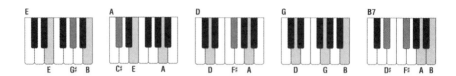

Intro ‖: E A | D A :‖ *Play 4 times*

       E A D A
Hey!

         E A D A
Unh-huh.

       E A D A
Hey!

         E A D
Unh-huh.

Verse 1   **A   E   D**
What I like about you,

        A   E A D A
You hold me tight.

E   A
Tell me I'm the only one,

D   A   E   A   D A
Wanna come over tonight.   Yeah!

© 1979 EMI APRIL MUSIC INC.
All Rights Reserved International Copyright Secured Used by Permission

	E A D A
Chorus 1	Keep on whispering in my ear,

               E   A   D   A
Tell me all the things that I wanna hear,

                                 E A
'Cause it's true.

               D   A   E   A   D
That's what I like about you.

	A E A
Verse 2	What I like about you,

               D   A   E   A   D
   You really know how to dance.

               A   E   A
When you go up, down, jump around,

               D   A   E   A   D   A
Think I've found true romance.   Yeah!

	E A D A
Chorus 2	Keep on whispering in my ear,

               E   A   D   A
Tell me all the things that I wanna hear,

                                 E A
'Cause it's true.

               D   A   E   A
That's what I like about you.

               D   A   E   A   D
That's what I like about you.

Interlude |G |D |G |A |
              |D   A |E   B7 | | |

Pre-Verse Repeat Intro

                   A   E   A   D
Verse 3   What I like about you,

                         A   E   A   D   A
               You keep me warm at night.

               E   A
               Never wanna let you go,

               D   A   E   A   D   A
               Know you make me feel alright.   Yeah!

               E   A   D   A
Chorus 3   Keep on whispering in my ear,

               E   A   D   A
               Tell me all the things that I wanna hear,

                           E   A
               'Cause it's true.

               D   A   E   A
                  That's what I like about you.

               D   A   E   A
                  That's what I like about you.

                D   A   E   A
               ‖: *That's what I like about you.*   :‖ *Play 4 times*

               D   A   N.C.
                     Hey!

Outro   ‖: E   A |D   A   :‖ *Repeat and fade (w/voc. ad lib)*

Wheel in the Sky

Words and Music by Robert Fleischman,
Neal Schon and Diane Valory

Melody:

Win-ter is here _ a - gain, _ oh Lord.

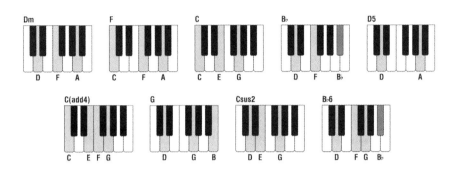

Intro   ‖: Dm   F | C   :‖   *Play 3 times*
          | B♭ | |
          | D5 | | | |

Verse 1

      D5
      Winter is here again, oh Lord.

                                C
Haven't been home in a year or more.

      C(add4)   D5
I hope she holds on a lit-tle longer.

Sent a letter on a long summer day

                   C
Made of silver not of clay.

      C(add4)   D5
Ooo, I've been runnin' down this dust-y road.

© 1978, 1980 TRIO MUSIC COMPANY, WEED-HIGH NIGHTMARE MUSIC and LACEY BOULEVARD MUSIC
All Rights for WEED-HIGH NIGHTMARE MUSIC Administered by WIXEN MUSIC PUBLISHING INC.
All Rights Reserved

Chorus 1

      D5   **F**   **C**
Oo, the wheel in the sky keeps on turnin'.

    D5   **F**   **C**
I don't know where I'll be tomorrow.

D5   **F**   **C**   **G** **Csus2** **C(add4)** **D5**
Wheel in the sky keeps on turnin'.

Verse 2

D5
    I been tryin' to make it home.

                    C
Got to make it before too long.

    C(add4)   **D5**
Oo, I can't take this very much longer.

I'm stranded in the sleet and rain.

                             C
Don't think I'm ever gonna make it home again.

      C(add4)
The morn - in' sun is risin',

D5
    It's kissin' the day.

	D5	F	C
Chorus 2	Oo, the wheel in the sky keeps on turnin'.		

Chorus 2

       D5   F   C
I don't know where I'll be tomorrow.

D5   F   C
Wheel in the sky keeps turnin'.

G   Csus2   C(add4)
Whoa,

G   Csus2   C(add4)
   My, my, my, my, my.

N.C.   D5
For tomorrow.

Solo   ‖: D5 | Csus2 :‖   *Play 3 times*
               ‖: B♭6 Csus2 | D5   Csus2 :‖
               | B♭6 | G   Csus2 |

Chorus 3

         D5   F   C
Oh, the wheel in the sky keeps on turnin'.

       D5   F   C
Oo, I don't know where I'll be to-morrow.

D5   F   C
Wheel in the sky keeps me yearnin'.

      G   Csus2   C(add4) D5
Oo, I don't know, I don't know.

Chorus 4   D5   F   C
         ‖: Oo, the wheel in the sky keeps on turnin'.

         D5   F   C
Oo, I don't know where I'll be to-morrow. :‖ *Play 4 times*

    ‖: B♭ | :‖ *Repeat and fade*

Will It Go Round in Circles

Words and Music by Billy Preston
and Bruce Fisher

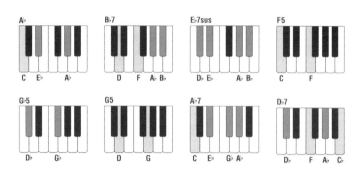

Verse 1

    Ab   Bb7 Eb7sus4
    I've got a song, I ain't got no melody.

    Ab   Bb7 Eb7sus4
    How'm I gonna sing it to my friends?

    Ab   Bb7 Eb7sus4
    I've got a song, I ain't got no melody.

    Ab
    How'm I gonna sing it to my friends?

Chorus 1

    F5   Gb5 G5 Ab7   Db7 Ab7
    Will it go round in   circles?

    Db7   Ab7   Db7 Ab7
    Will it fly high like a bird up in the sky?

    Db7   Ab7 Db7 Ab7
    Will it go round in circles?

    Db7   Ab7   Db7 Ab7 N.C.
    Will it fly high like a bird up in the sky?

Copyright © 1973 ALMO MUSIC CORP. and IRVING MUSIC, INC.
Copyright Renewed
All Rights Reserved   Used by Permission

Verse 2	A♭ B♭7 E♭7sus4 I've got a story, ain't got no moral.

Verse 2

A♭   B♭7 E♭7sus4
I've got a story, ain't got no moral.

A♭   B♭7 E♭7sus4
Let the bad guy win ev'ry once in a while.

A♭   B♭7 E♭7sus4
I've got a story, ain't got no moral.

A♭
Let the bad guy win ev'ry once in a while.

Chorus 2   *Repeat Chorus 1*

Verse 3

A♭   B♭7 E♭7sus4
I've got a dance, I ain't got no steps.

A♭   B♭7 E♭7sus4
I'm gonna let the music move me around.

A♭   B♭7 E♭7sus4
I've got a dance, I ain't got no steps.

A♭
I'm gonna let the music move me around.

Chorus 3   *Repeat Chorus 1*

Melodica Solo   *Repeat Verse 1 (Instrumental)*

Chorus 4   *Repeat Chorus 1*

Verse 4   *Repeat Verse 1*

Outro   *Repeat Chorus 1 till fade*

Wonderful Tonight

Words and Music by
Eric Clapton

It's late in the eve - ning;

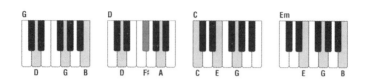

Intro | G | D | C | D |

Verse 1

G   D
It's late in the eve - ning;

C   D
She's wond'rin' what clothes__ to wear.

G   D
She puts on her make - up

C   D
And brushes her long__ blonde hair.

C   D
And then she asks__ me,

G   D   Em
"Do I look all right?"

         C
And I say, "Yes,

      D   G D C D
You look wonderful tonight."

Copyright © 1977 by Eric Patrick Clapton
Copyright Renewed
All Rights in the U.S. Administered by Unichappell Music Inc.
International Copyright Secured   All Rights Reserved

Verse 2

G   D
We go to a par - ty,

C   D
And ev'ryone turns__ to see

G   D
This beautiful la - dy

C   D
Is walking around__ with me.

C   D
And then she asks__ me,

G   D   Em
"Do you feel all right?"

       C
And I say, "Yes,

    D   G
I feel wonderful tonight."

Bridge

     C   D
I feel wonderful be-cause I see

    G   D   Em
The love__ light in__ your eyes.

     C   D
Then the wonder of it all

      C   D
Is that you just don't realize

      G D C D
How much I love__ you.

Verse 3

      G   **D**
It's time to go home__ now,

C   **D**
And I've got an aching head.

G   **D**
So I give her the car__ keys,

C   **D**
And she helps me to bed.

C   **D**
And then I tell__ her,

G   **D**   **Em**
As I turn out the light,

      C
I say, "My darling,

     D   **G** **D** **Em**
You are wonderful tonight.

D   **C**
Oh, my darling,

     D   **G** **D** **C** **D** **G**
You are wonderful tonight."

You're in My Heart

Words and Music by
Rod Stewart

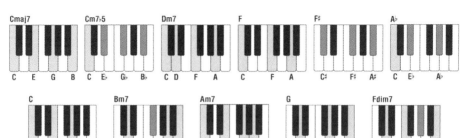

C E G	D F♯ A B	C E G A	D G B	D F A♭ C♭
C	Bm7	Am7	G	Fdim7

Intro | Cmaj7 | Cm7♭5 | Dm7 | F   F♯ G A♭ | C | | |

Verse 1

C   Bm7
   I didn't know what day it was

     Am7   G
When you walked into the room.

 C   Bm7
I said hello un-noticed,

    Am7   G
You said goodbye too soon.

C   Bm7
Breezin' through the clientele,

    Am7   G
Spinning yarns that were simply lyrical.

C   Bm7
  I really must con-fess right here,

    Am7   G   C   Bm7   Am7   G
The at-traction was purely physical.

Verse 2

C   Bm7
  I took all those habits of yours

     Am7   G
That in the be-ginning were hard to ac-cept.

© 1977 (Renewed 2005) ROD STEWART
All Rights Controlled and Administered by EMI APRIL MUSIC INC.
All Rights Reserved   International Copyright Secured   Used by Permission

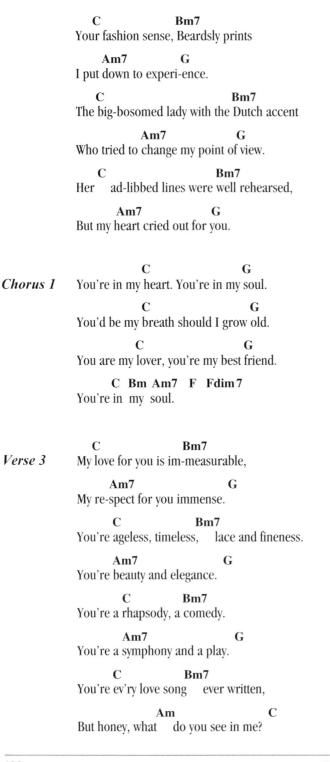

C   Bm7
Your fashion sense, Beardsly prints

 Am7   G
I put down to experi-ence.

 C   Bm7
The big-bosomed lady with the Dutch accent

  Am7   G
Who tried to change my point of view.

  C   Bm7
Her ad-libbed lines were well rehearsed,

  Am7   G
But my heart cried out for you.

Chorus 1

    C   G
You're in my heart. You're in my soul.

    C   G
You'd be my breath should I grow old.

    C   G
You are my lover, you're my best friend.

   C Bm Am7 F Fdim 7
You're in my soul.

Verse 3

  C   Bm7
My love for you is im-measurable,

  Am7   G
My re-spect for you immense.

   C   Bm7
You're ageless, timeless, lace and fineness.

  Am7   G
You're beauty and elegance.

   C   Bm7
You're a rhapsody, a comedy.

   Am7   G
You're a symphony and a play.

   C   Bm7
You're ev'ry love song ever written,

    Am   C
But honey, what do you see in me?

Chorus 2   **Repeat Chorus 1**

               C
Verse 4   You're an essay in glamor.

       Bm7
Please pardon the grammar,

          Am   **G**
But you're ev'ry schoolboy's dream.

        C   **Bm7**
You're Celtic united, but baby I've decided

         Am7   **G**
You're the best team I've ever seen.

C   **Bm7**
   And there have been many affairs

        Am7   **G**
And many times I've felt to leave.

C   **Bm7**
But I bite my lip and   turn around,

         Am7   **G**
'Cause you're the warmest thing I've ever found.

          C   **G**
Chorus 3   You're in my heart. You're in my soul.

          C   **G**
You'd be my breath should I grow old.

          C   **G**
You are my lover, you're my best friend.

       C **Bm** **Am7**   **G**
You're in my soul.

You Are So Beautiful

Words and Music by Billy Preston
and Bruce Fisher

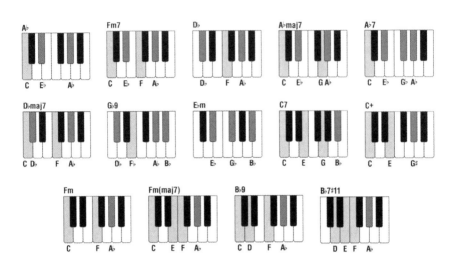

Intro   ‖: A♭ | Fm7   D♭   :‖

Verse 1

A♭   A♭maj7   A♭7   D♭maj7   G♭9
   You are_____ so____ beautiful

  A♭   A♭7
To me.

A♭   A♭maj7   A♭7   D♭maj7   G♭9
You are_____ so____ beautiful

  A♭   A♭maj7
To me.

Copyright © 1973 IRVING MUSIC, INC. and ALMO MUSIC CORP.
Copyright Renewed
All Rights Reserved   Used by Permission

       Ebm Ab7
Can't you see?

Dbmaj7   C7   C+ C7
    You're ev'rything I hope for.

Fm   Fm(maj7) Fm7   Bb9
    You're__ ev'ry - thing I need.

Ab   Abmaj7 Ab7 Dbmaj7   Gb9
   You are_____ so_____beautiful

    Ab Abmaj7
To me.

Verse 2   Ab   Abmaj7 Ab7 Dbmaj7   Gb9
    You are_____ so___ beautiful

    Ab Ab7
To me.

Ab Abmaj7 Ab7   Dbmaj7   Gb9
You are_____ so___ beautiful

    Ab Abmaj7
To me.

       Ebm Ab7
Can't you see?

Dbmaj7   C7   C+ C7
    You're ev'rything I hope for.

Fm   Bb7#11
    Ev'rything I need.

Ab   Abmaj7 Ab7 Dbmaj7   Gb9
   You are_____ so___ beautiful

    Ab   Abmaj7 Ab7 Dbmaj7 Gb9 Ab
To__ me.

You've Got a Friend

Words and Music by
Carole King

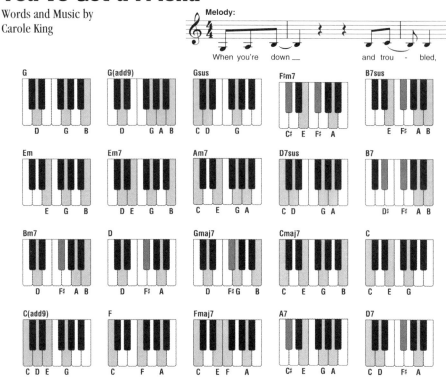

Intro | G G(add9) Gsus | C/D | Gsus G G(add9) G | F#m7 B7sus

Verse 1

        B7   Em   B7
When you're down__ and trou - bled,

        Em   B7   Em Em7
And you need a helping hand,

      Am7   D7sus   G Gsus G Gsus G
And nothing, whoa, nothing is goin' right,

F#m7   B7
Close your eyes and think of me,

      Em   B7   Em Em7
And soon I will__ be there

      Am7   Bm7   D7sus D
To brighten up even your darkest night.

© 1971 (Renewed 1999) COLGEMS-EMI MUSIC INC.
All Rights Reserved   International Copyright Secured   Used by Permission

Chorus 1

          G   **Gmaj7**
You just call__ out my name,

          Cmaj7   **Am7**
And you know wherever I am

D7sus   **G**   **Gmaj7**
I'll come run - ning, oh yeah, babe,

                    D7sus
To see you again.

G   **Gmaj7**
Winter, spring, summer or fall,

        Cmaj7   **Em7**
Now, all you got to do is call,

         Cmaj7 **Bm7**   **C/D D7sus**
And I'll be there,__ yeah, yeah, yeah.

                    G G(add9) G C   **G**   **F#m7 B7sus**
You've got a friend.

Verse 2

          B7   **Em**   **B7**
If the sky__ above__ you

            Em   **B7**   **Em** **Em7**
Should turn__ dark and full of clouds,

        Am7   **D7sus**   **G Gsus G**
And that old North wind should begin to blow,

F#m7   **B7**
  Keep your head togeth - er

      Em   **B7**   **Em Em7 Am7**
And call my name__ out loud, now.

          Bm7   **D7sus**
Soon I'll be knock - in' upon your door.

Chorus 2

C(add9)   Gmaj7

You just call___ out my name,

Cmaj7   Am7

And you know___ wherever I am,

D7sus   G   Gsus   G

I'll come run - ning,   oh yes, I will,

                 D7sus

To see you again.

G   Gmaj7

Winter, spring, summer or fall,

   Cmaj7   Em7

Yeah, all you got to do is call,

       Cmaj7   Bm7   C/D D7sus

And I'll be there, yeah,___ yeah, yeah.

Bridge

          C/F   F

Hey, ain't___ it good to know

     C/D

That you've got a friend

      G   Gsus   Gmaj7

When people can be___ so cold?

      C

They'll hurt you,

       Fmaj7

And desert you.

       Em   Em7   A7

Well, they'll take your soul if you let___ them,

          D7sus   D7

Oh yeah, but don't___ you let them.

              Gmaj7

Chorus 3   You just call__ out my name,

        Cmaj7   **Am7**

And you know wherever I am,

D7sus   **G**   **Gsus** **G**

   I'll come run-ning

                  D7sus

To see you again.

Oh, babe, don't you know 'bout

G   **Gmaj7**

Winter, spring, summer or fall,

      Cmaj7   **Em7**

Hey, now all you've got to do is call.

        Cmaj7   **Bm7**   **C/D** **D7sus**

Lord, I'll be__ there, yes, I will.

               G **G(add9)** **G** **C**

Outro   You've got a friend.

               G

You've got a friend, yeah.

C   **G**

   Ain't it good to know you've got__ a friend?

      C

Ain't it good to know

               Gsus **G** **G(add9)** **G**

You've got a friend?

      C   **Gsus** **G** **G(add9)** **G**

Oh,__ yeah, yeah. You've got a friend.

You're the Inspiration

Words and Music by Peter Cetera
and David Foster

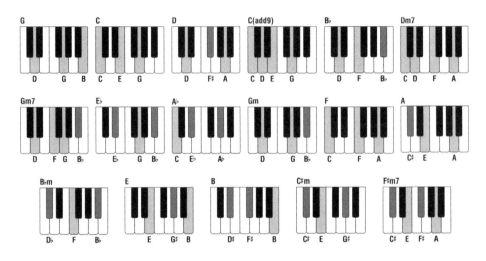

Intro | G   C | D   G | C(add9) | D |

Verse 1

  B♭   **Dm7**
   You know our love was meant to be

  Gm7   **E♭** **F**
   The kind of love that lasts for-ever.

  B♭   **Dm7**
   And I want you here with me

  Gm7   **E♭**
   From tonight until the end__ of time.

  F   **B♭ E♭**   **A♭**
 You should know__ ev'rywhere I go;

  D   **Gm** **C**   **F**
 Always on my mind,__ in my heart,

  D   **G A**
 In my soul,__ baby.

Copyright © 1984 by Universal Music - MGB Songs and Foster Frees Music, Inc.
International Copyright Secured   All Rights Reserved

Chorus 1

D
You're the meaning of my life,

G   D A
You're the inspi - ra - tion.

D
You bring feeling to my life,

G   D A
You're the inspi - ra - tion.

F   C
Wanna have you near me,

B♭   B♭m
I wanna have you hear me saying

F   B♭   C F B♭ E♭ F
No one needs you more than I need you.

Verse 2

B♭
And I know (Yes, I know.)

                 Dm7
That it's plain to see

Gm7   E♭   F
We're so in love when we're to-gether.

B♭
Now I know (Now I know.)

                 Dm7
That I need you here with me

Gm7   E♭
From tonight to the end__ of time.

F   B♭ E♭   A♭
You should know__ ev'rywhere I go;

D   Gm   C   F
Always on my mind,__ you're in my heart,

D   G A
In my soul.

Chorus 2

D
You're the meaning of my life,

G   D A
You're the inspi - ra - tion.

D
　　　You bring feeling to my life,

G　　　　　**D**　**A**
You're the inspi - ra - tion.

F　　　　　　　**C**
　　Wanna have you near me,

　B♭　　　　　　　**B♭m**
I wanna have you hear me saying

F　　　**B♭**　　　　　　　**A**　**D**
　　No one needs you more than I need　you.

Interlude　‖: **D**　　　‖ **G**　　**D**　**A**　:‖

Bridge
F　　　　　　**C**
　　Wanna have you near me,

　B♭　　　　　　　**B♭m**
I wanna have you hear me say, yeah,

F　　　**B♭**　　　　　　　**C**　**A**
　　No one needs you more than I need you.

Chorus 3
E
You're the meaning of my life,

A　　　　　**E**　**B**
You're the inspi - ra - tion.

E　　　　　　**C♯m**
　　You bring feeling to my life,

A　　　**E**　**F♯m7**　**B**
You're the inspi - ra - tion.

Outro
　　　　　　　　E
‖: When you love somebody.

E　　　　　**A**　　**E**　**B**
(Till the end of time.)

　　　　E
When you love somebody,

C♯m　　　　**A**
(Always on my mind.)

　　　　　　E　**F♯m7**　　**B**
No one needs__ you more than I.　:‖　*Repeat and fade*